# UNLEASHED!

JUSTIN FORD

© 2022 Justin Ford

All rights reserved. No part of this book may be reproduced or transmitted in any form or by any means including, but not limited to, electronic or mechanical, photocopying, recording, or by any information storage and retrieval system without written permission from the publisher, except for the inclusion of brief quotations in review.

Author:              Ford, Justin
Cover Designer:      Lorenzo Edwards

First U.S. Edition 2022 Soft cover, Perfect Bound
Publisher's Cataloging-In-Publication Data

*Ford, Justin*

*Unleashed*

Summary: The book *Unleashed!,* by Justin Ford is a perfect road map for this current time in the world. The word "Purpose" can be daunting at times, but this book gives you a tangible, biblical guide to both find it and keep it. It is a true testament to Gods Faithfulness and promises over our lives. This book has inspired me to set my goals higher, trust God's voice, trust the process, forgive past transgressions, fast more often and live a *Unleashed* life.

Library of Congress Control Number: 2022900766

For current information about releases by Justin Ford visit his website at justinfordunleashed.com.

Printed in the United States of America
v7.4 2-14-2022

When I met Justin it was clear to me he had achieved something at a young age that is extraordinary. What I wasn't prepared for was the story of how he got there. When you put the old Justin into the story you see a miracle. Justin's journey of transformation is a blueprint for anyone who wants to reverse the curse of poverty and self destruction. The turning point in his life is something you don't want to miss. It was a supernatural encounter with God and a boot camp! The combination produced 8 principles that will transform any life! Give God permission to put you into His boot camp and you're destined to end up like Justin with a life that other people look at and say "I wish that was my life."

- Lance Wallnau,
Speaker, Author, CEO at Lance Learning Group

Justin really speaks from the heart throughout this entire book. What I love about Justin is his real and raw approach to sharing what it takes to be successful. There's no fluff and certainly no sugar coating anything with Justin and anyone who reads this book will be better personally and professionally after completing it.

- Jeff Glover,
Founder & CEO of the Live Unreal Companies, Glover U, & Jeff Glover & Associates

*Unleashed!* is a burst of power releasing the kind of God-faith that changes us from the inside out. I've truly enjoyed my front-row seat in Justin's life. Not only can I affirm the miracle, but I will testify to the power of these truths. If this book is in your hands, then your life is in God's hands and He is ready to change it in marvelous ways.

- Patrick Bossio, Jr.,
Senior Pastor CHRISTfamily Church, Brownstown, MI

This book will change your life! Justin Ford does an exemplary job not only sharing fundamental principles that will catapult you into your destiny—he refreshingly does it through excellent transparency and vulnerability. I am one who speaks into Justin's life. I have seen firsthand his approach to changing any difficulty or situation in his life. He does the work and clearly spells out that process in Unleashed. As you read this book, I am confident that God will unlock inside of you what you need to understand how important you are to God and that He has a promise and a future for you. Have pen and paper ready! Justin not only shares his story, more importantly, he asks prodding questions and gives you poignant assignments that will help you identify where you are—and by the end of the book— you'll see where you are going. I highly value authentic leaders who share their stories and, more importantly, live out what they say to others. That's valuable. That's who Justin is.

–Cindy Williams Moore,
Spiritual Executive Coach & Prophet

Justin Ford has created a practical template for your success in his new book, **UNLEASHED**. With refreshing candor and vulnerability, he used his own story of misfortune, hardship and bad choices as a backdrop to describe the keys that turned his life around. With **UNLEASHED**, Justin will become a mentor to you as you journey into the life God longs for you to have!

- Eric Williams,
Pastor & Entrepreneur

The book *Unleashed,* by Justin Ford is a perfect road map for this current time in the world. The word "Purpose" can be daunting at times, but this book gives you a tangible, Biblical guide to both find it and keep it. It is a true testament to God's faithfulness and promises over our lives. This book has inspired me to set my goals higher, trust God's voice, trust the process, forgive past transgressions, fast more often and live and *Unleashed* life.

- Dave Rayner,
Former NFL player, Real Estate Agent

"*Unleashed*" is a book Justin Ford wrote to help people be defined by their destiny, rather than their history. I have watched, invested and prayed with Justin as he has walked out and written this prescription of 8 principles for life advancement. Truly all things are possible for those…for you…for all who read, believe and allow Christ to empower us to live His life in us successfully.—

- Arthur Ledlie,
CEO Bridge Networks | Embassy Training Center
Fire House Prayer | Global Impact

Justin Ford's book, **Unleashed** embodies thousands of years of applicable wisdom along with the guidance to apply it in our lives today. Anyone who is searching for a more meaningful and impactful life must read this book. His transparency is painfully real, but in a world filled with mock reality and vanity it is like fresh water in a barren desert. In leaving it all on the table for his readers it allows us to see a true case study in the redemptive qualities proposed in the book. This is not a read that will merely leave you with a few metaphorical questions about life to ponder. Instead it makes you take a serious inventory of your inner most being and then provides clear action steps to start living with meaning and impact TODAY!

- Andy Dirks,
Former MLB Player, Real Estate Agent

Some books inform the reader, while others encourage and inspire; but there are yet other writings that depict the life's journey of the author. Very few books, however, are all-encompassing and contain all of the elements of the aforementioned. This book, "***Unleashed***", by Justin Ford is one of those unique writings that is indeed all-encompassing. As Justin shares some of the riveting elements of his life, the reader gets a clear sense that the Holy Spirit was posturing him to be catapulted into a new dimension of kingdom purpose. I'm particularly struck by his candor, transparency, and his capacity to convey, "the good, the bad, and the ugly." As I continued reading, chapter after chapter, it reminded me of the 'teleological" nature of the grace of our God. Don't let that seemingly weighty theological term throw you. It simply means that which is related to or is involved with the explanation of a series of events or occurrences and the purpose they serve, rather than the cause by which they arise. The Biblical passage that mostly speaks to this concept is Romans 8:28 (NKJV) which states, "all things work together for good to those who love God, to those who are the called according to His purpose." I have known Justin for over ten years, and in the last few years, I've had the honor to serve as his apostolic leader by virtue of him being a part of our local Ekklesia. I have a deep appreciation for his passion for the things of God, as well as his commitment to his wife Joy, and their four children, and one grandchild. I strongly endorse Justin Ford's new book "***Unleashed,***" and I believe the seven principles with the eighth bonus principal, which he so succinctly communicates, will not only inspire and encourage you, but also provide a clear pathway on how to authentically overcome obstacles and disappointments, and use them as a platform to "Unleash" you into your new day of destiny."

- Ellis L. Smith,
Apostolic Overseer Jubilee City Church

Wow! Justin's has a true rock bottom to redemption story! We have all faced adversity at some level in our lives and his "**8 Key Principles**" are Biblical wisdom that will bless you and make sure that you not only overcome adversity, but also thrive in every area of your life. His story will inspire you and the practical principles will guide you. This incredible book will be one that you will find yourself coming back to over and over again when life throws you a curve ball.

- Dr. Jason Olafsson,
Founder and CEO of Custom Health Centers

By prayer and my faith, it is my hope that this book by Justin Ford, Unleashes the potential of millions of God's people. I am grateful that Justin humbled himself to share in detail about the devil's plan to destroy his life and how God's amazing redemptive power, grace and favor completely turned his life around. ***Unleashed*** does an amazing job explaining a Biblical and practical strategy for anybody and everybody to turn their life around and fulfill their God given mission. A must read and a great gift!

- Asaad Faraj,
Senior National Sales Director Primerica

Read this book and change! Justin Ford designed "***Unleased,***" with you in mind. Let these real accounts in Justin's life be your school as you learn. Justin's personal experience is evidence that he has already paid your tuition. This compelling story is your invitation to take this important class for free. It is proof that God has a destiny for you too. Author, Justin Ford, is a living example of the power of Romans 8:28. Please be open to his wisdom. When you are not open to wisdom, you force pain to become your only teacher!

-Dr. James Foster,
Foster Your Life, LLC

Justin Ford is a walking miracle and a living testament of God's redemptive power. As you read this book you will be moved by his transparency in giving the details of the depth of darkness he once lived in, and testimony of God's miraculous intervention that saved his life from destruction. This book will inspire you to believe that a born again experience is possible even in situations that seem hopeless. His comeback and turn around, reminds us all that our faith is built upon a power that can transforms lives and take them from dark to light, and death to life. I am honored to call Justin my friend, brother and co-laborer in building the Kingdom of God in the earth. He has become a successful businessman, husband, father, minister, and a great example of Christ like character. This book needs to be widely distributed all over the world spreading the message of God's amazing love.

- Timothy Alden,
Pastor of The Movement Global,
Author of "The Purity Revolution"

# UNLEASHED!

### BY JUSTIN FORD

# DEDICATION

I want to dedicate this book to my late Grandpa John J. Murphy. Although I wasn't his biological grandson, he always treated me like I was. He always believed in me, even in my troubled days. Grandpa, you'll never know how much of an impact you made on my life. I wish you could see the man I am today. I still have the rock you gave me for Christmas with the words on it that read as follows, "Accept the challenges so that you may feel the exhilaration of Victory." This has helped me through so much! Miss you and love you!

# ACKNOWLEDGMENTS

I want to start by thanking the most important person in my life, my Lord and Savior Jesus Christ. Without You I am nothing and would have never been able to write this book if You didn't save me. Thank You! To the second most important person in my life, my wife, Joy! Thank you for loving me, believing in me, and persevering with me even through the tough times. To my four children, Angelina, Emilio, Tiara, and Judah. You four mean the world to me and I am blessed to be your Dad. To my grandson Joel the III, I pray that I would be able to have the impact on your life that my Grandpa had on mine. To all of the people along my journey that have helped me and played a role in getting me to this point, thank you! Thank you Sabrina Adams for staying on me and helping me with my book. Although it took over two years, We made it! And a big thank you to Natasha Lappos for helping me edit my book and making it ready for the world to read! I pray my story and the principles in this book impact and help millions of people around the world live an *Unleashed* life!

# TABLE OF CONTENTS

Introduction..................................................................................... 17

Chapter 1 Principle One – Discovering Your Purpose......................... 39
Chapter 2 Principle Two – Create A Vision............................................ 51
Chapter 3 Principle Three - Forgiveness................................................. 63
Chapter 4 Principle Four – Freedom From Fear.................................... 71
Chapter 5 Principle Five – Understand and Trust The Process............ 81
Chapter 6 Principle Six – Mentorship & Accountability....................... 91
Chapter 7 Principle Seven – Humility, The Doorway To Destiny........ 99
Chapter 8 Bonus Principle 8 – The Secret Weapon................................107
In Closing..................................................................................................113

Author Bio "Justin Ford".........................................................................115

## INTRODUCTION
## UNLEASHED

*To suddenly release a violent force that cannot be controlled: to let happen or begin something powerful that, once begun, cannot be controlled. To release from or as if from a leash; set loose to pursue or run at will. To free from restraint or control*

# Seven Key Principles to Breaking Free and Breaking Through

## Introduction

You were created for an amazing purpose. You were created to complete a very specific assignment here on earth that only YOU can fulfill. No matter what you have gone through, are currently going through, or are yet to go through doesn't matter. What you are going through right now may seem to contradict your purpose. That doesn't change God's calling for your life. Regardless of what anyone has told you, your life matters and God loves you MORE than you could ever imagine!

In this book, I'll share with you my story. You'll find out how I went from rock-bottom to being Unleashed! I will give you the Seven Key Principles that I've applied to my life that have allowed me to flourish personally and professionally.

Believe me, they work. I've gone from high school dropout to successful entrepreneur, drug dealer to a motivational speaker. I went from a struggling alcoholic to husband and father. I went from hurting people to helping people succeed and teaching them to live a life of success, purpose, and fulfillment.

You may not have experienced drug and alcohol abuse. You might not have a dramatic story like mine. Your fight may be entirely different, like depression, sex addiction, gambling, anxiety, or fear. Whatever it is, if it has a controlling grip over you—the cycle is the same.

I've written this book to share the good news with you. Like me, you too can break free and experience liberty, happiness, and joy!

You can be ultimately "**UNLEASHED**" into all that God has created you to be! Let me tell you, what He has in-store for you is AMAZING!

I firmly believe that everything I went through, all the hard times, dark days, and struggles—as terrible as they were—God has used and allowed me to share my story with you. Why? So that you can know beyond all doubt that with God, ALL THINGS ARE POSSIBLE! There is hope if you are experiencing hopelessness, there is light beyond the darkness, and there is freedom if you are bound by addiction or anything else that is holding you back.

First, I will dive into my story and give lots of background information. In the second section of the book, I'll outline the seven key principles that I have applied to my life, and I will give you practical examples of how you can get started.

### Trigger Alert

*My story is rough. It contains lots of emotional pain, substance abuse, and crime. If you're sensitive to such topics, prepare yourself. I've done my best here to relay the facts and communicate my experience—but let me be clear—I'm neither exaggerating nor glorifying my misconduct. Reading it might be difficult, and I'm sorry for that, but my goal is to keep it real. I want to be transparent because I know there are others like me out there that need to hear this and know it's possible to break free and come out on the other side.*

# INTRODUCTION
## EARLY LIFE AND UPBRINGING

I believe what you experience in your childhood directly impacts your adolescent years, teen years, and on through adulthood. We often don't understand why we struggle with issues like rejection, insecurity, fear, or depression. I believe it's due to experiences from childhood that get lodged into our growing conscious and subconscious minds. Being so young, we don't yet have the faculties to adequately process these events, so they remain. Often, we don't even know they are there. They've become part of the furniture, so to speak. Although my childhood wasn't particularly bad, some things happened that caused lots of emotional pain and trauma.

My parents married at 22 years old. I was born seven months later, and my sister 15 months after that. They divorced when I was two years old. I can't remember anything before that, but I know for a fact their divorce affected me. Divorce negatively impacts children, no matter how you slice it. Parents and home-life areas affect the whole fabric of a child's understanding. Ripping apart a family for a child is akin to ripping apart their reality. Perhaps this was my first time encountering the fear of abandonment. No longer seeing my Dad come home every night was tricky—I remember the feeling. I was only two years old, but I still remember the pain.

My mom remarried shortly afterward, and we moved to Detroit. My stepdad was a good guy and treated me well. He already had a daughter, and soon my mom had my little sister. I was outnumbered. Growing up with three sisters was isolating. I still made the best of it, and like any good brother, I purposely annoyed and picked on my sisters. I'd often get in trouble or grounded. My stepdad made time to connect and spend time with me, but I always missed my Dad. I didn't see him as much as I would have liked during those years.

My adolescent years were, for the most part, very good. We were a low-to-middle class family, and I was a regular young boy. I played lots of sports, rode bikes, built forts, and aggravated the neighbors. I got into trouble here and there but nothing major. I tried cigarettes for the first time at 11 years old and kissed a girl for the first time a year later.

My mom's marriage seemed to be going well until it abruptly ended. I did not know what caused it or understood what was going on for the first few days. My whole family split—and quickly. Now 12 years old, I went to live with my Dad, my full-sister remained with my mom, my half-sister stayed with my stepdad, and my stepsister went to live with her aunt and uncle.

Unfortunately, I couldn't keep a strong relationship with my sisters. We still speak occasionally but lived apart during some of our most formative years. It's a shame. Experiencing the fallout of that divorce served to feed my mounting insecurities and fear. I'd feel the real consequences soon enough.

## THE SLIPPERY SLOPE

The first few years with my Dad went as well as they could have given the circumstances. Dad was a busy and short-tempered man. So I focused on school and staying out of his way. But in the summer of 1999 and the months that followed, my life quickly spun out of control.

I was 16 years old and living life to the fullest. I had a great summer job, a ton of friends, and a bright future. I had just been accepted to a prestigious and exclusive program at the Michigan Summer Institute (SI). It was for aspiring law students to experience college life. My grandfather was an attorney. He wrote me a killer letter of recommendation and was so pleased to hear I'd been accepted. He'd promised to pass on his law firm to me if I continued in law and became a lawyer. There was one condition, he told me that I had to stay out of trouble with the law or else I wouldn't be able to go to law school. I was so excited and motivated to get started. The experience was great too! I met a great group of friends, and we all stayed in dorms, attended classes, and ate in the cafeteria. I truly got a taste of what college life would be like. I was so excited for my future! Sadly, I had no way of knowing that would be my only college experience.

Upon my return from the SI program, my life quickly changed. One afternoon I walked into the local gas station to purchase some cigarettes (would you believe I'd begun smoking habitually at 14?).

# INTRODUCTION

I instantly noticed the new, young, and very attractive girl behind the counter. She noticed me too. We chatted away, and I found out she lived close by, in my same apartment complex. She was older, 19—I was only 16. I still asked for her number. She gave it to me, and well, the rest is history.

It wasn't long before she became my entire world. All my focus was on her and hooking up with her at every available opportunity. A few short months later, once I turned 17, I moved out of my Dad's house and into an apartment with her. I was still in the 11th grade but had quickly lost all interest in school or ever becoming an attorney. I was having too much fun staying up late, smoking cigarettes, getting high, drinking, and having sex whenever I wanted. I was living a rock star's lifestyle (so I thought), and I didn't want to wake up to go to school in the morning. I went from being an honor roll student to a dropout within a few short months.

But my newfound life quickly spiraled out of control. My girlfriend and I fought constantly. Our relationship was not healthy, and it often became rather violent. We both got arrested and charged with domestic violence. I didn't know then that the county jail would be a regular stop for me over the following 18 months.

Things began to turn for the worse once I found out my girlfriend was pregnant. I wish I could say I manned up and fixed my ways, but that wasn't the case. Things got worse.

I'm sure you've heard marijuana referred to as a gateway drug; it's the gate into harsher and stronger narcotics. I didn't believe that was the case until I walked headlong through that gate. By the time I was 18, I was already into Cocaine, Ecstasy, and many other drugs—I was selling them as well.

I had begun hanging with an older crowd. We would go to clubs every weekend, drink alcohol, and use drugs on a regular. We would begin partying Thursday evening and sometimes it wouldn't end until past midnight on Sunday. I once stayed up for five days straight on drugs without any sleep or food and almost died. That was my cycle. I'd party like there' was no tomorrow, get as high as I could, then feel like I was dying on the way down. I

**UNLEASHED**, by Justin Ford

often prayed and asked God to please change my life and get me out of this cycle, as I felt trapped and didn't know how to get free.

Remember I told you that jail became a regular stop? Within two years, I acquired eight misdemeanors, a felony, and was arrested a total of 13 times on drug and alcohol-related charges. My felony? I sold drugs to an undercover cop (see below mug shot).

## OAKLAND COUNTY
## SHERIFF'S OFFICE
## MUGSHOT PROFILE

| | |
|---|---|
| NAME: | FORD JUSTIN SCOTT |
| AKA: | |
| AKA: | |
| AKA: | |
| AKA: | |
| INMATE#: | 285286 |
| BOOKING#: | 392787 |
| OCS BOOKING DATE: | 10/09/01 |
| OCS BOOKING TIME: | 21:27 |
| DATE OF BIRTH: | |
| SOCIAL SECURITY#: | |
| SID#: | |
| FBI#: | |
| DRIVERS STATE: | MICHIGAN |
| DRIVERS LIC#: | |

**PHYSICAL DESCRIPTION**

| | |
|---|---|
| SEX: | MALE |
| RACE: | WHITE |
| HEIGHT: | 510 |
| WEIGHT: | 170 |
| HAIR COLOR: | BLOND OR STRAWB |
| HAIR LENGTH: | SHORT |
| FACIAL HAIR: | NONE |
| EYE COLOR: | BROWN |
| EYE CHARACTERISTICS: | NORMAL |
| GLASSES: | NO |
| BUILD: | MEDIUM |
| COMPLEXION: | MEDIUM |
| TEETH: | NORMAL/STRAIGHT |

SCARS/MARKS/TATTOOS

#1:
#2:
#3:
#4:
#5:

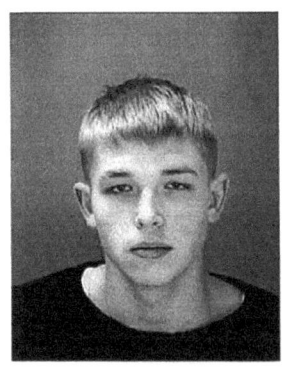
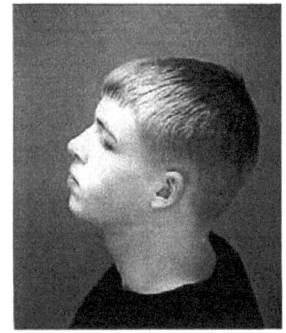

# INTRODUCTION

My friends and I were partying before a concert in Pontiac, Michigan. I was already high and drunk. I had a pocket full of Ecstasy; I planned on selling it. I had already begun regularly selling Ecstasy at clubs. It provided all the funds I needed to continue my lifestyle. I had two friends with me, and some guys approached us and asked if we had any drugs to sell. One of my friends leaned in and whispered he knew these guys were undercover cops and not to sell. I didn't listen; I made the deal and walked off. Within minutes we were surrounded by police cars and thrown to the ground, and as you can imagine, my friends were livid.

All three of us were taken to jail and put in separate cells. Surprisingly, we were let out the following day and told that charges were pending the drug lab analysis by the state police. By then, I was already on probation in three other cities due to two minor possession of alcohol charges, a drunken disorderly and a drunk driving!

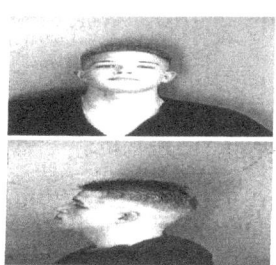

## UNLEASHED, by Justin Ford

One of my minor possession charges was rather eventful. It started when our party was too loud and disturbed the neighbors. The cops showed up and warned us that if they needed to come back, everyone would be arrested. Well, they came back and followed through with their warning. We decided we wouldn't let them in and barricaded the door with a couch. They came in through the windows. I ran upstairs and attempted to hide under a big pile of dirty laundry in my friend's room. Gun drawn; the officer told me to get up. We were all handcuffed and arrested in my friend's living room.

The officers were very upset with us. First, they had to come back, and second, they needed to call back up and enter through the windows. (Thinking back on it now, I wonder if that was even legal…anyway, it's just a thought.) As the officers held us in the living room, I began mouthing off. I got slapped—hard. This wasn't new behavior for me. Every time I'd be under the influence of some substance, I'd get really belligerent and act foolishly. If I was drunk, I wouldn't remember my behavior the next day.

I continued to run my mouth at the cops all the way to the station. They must have sent a message ahead because a group of them were waiting outside for me. While handcuffed, they pulled me out of the car and roughed me up a bit. My ribs were hurt badly, and my head got banged up against a brick wall. My eye got split open and began to bleed rather profusely. They told me I needed stitches, but I refused. The scar is still visible.

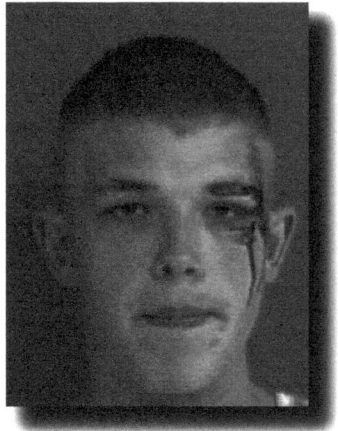 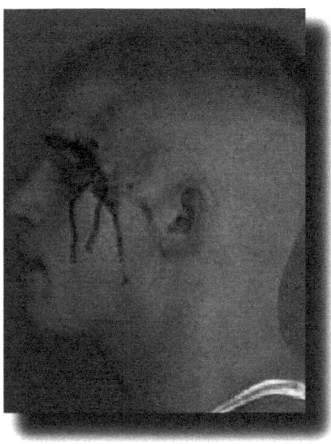

# INTRODUCTION

This was the state of my life at the time. I never wanted the party to stop. I was always looking for another drink of alcohol, more drugs, the next high, a girl to sleep with, and more party-goers. I would oftentimes find myself as the last man standing because I never wanted to come down from the high. I couldn't tell you then why the high was so appealing, but looking back now it was very obvious because I didn't want to focus on or fix my problems. When I was high I felt like I was Superman, and it got me into a lot of trouble and it nearly cost me my life multiple times.

## ROCK BOTTOM

One night I had been drinking and using cocaine. I hadn't slept and got picked by an older friend I knew with a few girls around 7:00 a.m. We drove around drinking and getting high and we ended up getting into an argument. That wasn't unexpected. I was always running my mouth. He kicked me out of his truck at a gas station in Royal Oak early in the morning. I was beyond drunk, higher than a kite, and caused a scene. Someone called the police. I was arrested and charged with public intoxication also known as drunken disorderly. I remember sitting in the jail cell so dehydrated I thought I would die. Delusional and desperate, I drank the water out of the toilet bowl of the jail cell to try and stay hydrated because the police officers refused to give me anything to drink.

That was my rock bottom or so I thought. You would think after an experience like that, I would surely change.

How did I get to this point in my life at only 19 years old?

I felt enslaved. I didn't know how to break free from this lifestyle but I knew for sure I didn't want it anymore. I look back now and see very clearly I was riding on the highway to hell. Like I did many times before, I prayed and asked God to please help me. Coming down from the high felt like death and I knew if I continued in this way it would overtake me and that I probably would die.

My mom would often say she was awaiting the day she'd get the call from the coroner to identify my body. The way I was living, that wasn't an unreasonable expectation. I could write a whole book of incidents that took place on my path to destruction, but I won't, and never will. It wasn't glamorous, it was sad. I just wanted to give you a taste of the madness and hopelessness of it all. Thankfully, my story doesn't end there—*in the jail cell toilet bowl.*

## CINCO DE MAYO

May 5th, 2002, (a.k.a. Cinco De Mayo) my life changed forever. It was Sunday and I woke up ready and excited to go to church. My life was turning around. I had gotten a steady server job at Rio Bravo Restaurant. I had started attending church on the regular and had gotten Baptized. That morning I remember my mom telling me how proud she was. She had let me move in to help me get my life back on track, and I was so thankful. As she handed me the keys to her car she said, "I trust you—don't ruin my trust." I told her I wouldn't, and left for church.

As I arrived at church, I remember the sound of the choir singing. The atmosphere was so energetic. I remember feeling a sense of freedom and newness of life that I had never felt before. At the altar during prayer time, I prayed, "God, I wish I could experience church like this every day." I did not know just how quickly He would answer my prayer.

I left the church and headed to the restaurant. I was on a spiritual high. The atmosphere at the restaurant was buzzing too. Everyone was getting ready for the biggest party of the year, Cinco De Mayo. Tents were set up in the parking lot, and a DJ was brought in. The music was thumping and my spiritual high quickly dissipated.

I was a new Christian, and old habits die hard. The bartender and I came up with a plan. In the chaos of it all, no one was keeping too close attention to us, so we decided to pocket the cash from drinks and split it at the end of the day. We figured we'd each pocket several hundred dollars.

# INTRODUCTION

With the restaurant at capacity and the party in full effect, I found myself overwhelmed by the temptation to party and drink. Before I knew it, I was kicking back long Island ice teas (three to four in the matter of an hour) in the bathroom. The atmosphere was just like a Friday night at the club. It was all too familiar, and I got swept up in the party.

I began to act belligerent to the customers. One customer complained to management. I was called into the office and almost fired. I was surprised my manager didn't know I had been drinking. I was given one more chance to get myself together—this wasn't the first time I'd been in trouble. You can probably guess what happened next.

I didn't get it together—I unraveled. Not long after my talk with the manager, I was caught drinking margaritas with customers in the parking lot. I got dragged to the office again and fired on the spot. It was 3:00 p.m., on a Sunday, and I was beyond drunk. Barely conscious, I got into my mom's car and left. Just a few hours earlier I promised her she could trust me with her car. What was I thinking? From there I decided to go downtown Detroit and visit the club;

I had to keep the party going. I vaguely remember stopping off at a party store and having someone purchase some beer for me. Blacking in and out I finally arrived at the club that evening. Shortly afterward I was kicked out for underage drinking. So I went back to my mom's car and finished off my beer.

Crazy thing is, on my way back to the car I met a homeless man and invited him into the car to drink with me. I began telling him all about how I was making a change in my life, and I was following God. I was talking about following God to a stranger while completely and utterly drunk. Cue eye-roll.

After the man left, I drove over to Greektown in Detroit. I planned on getting a job in that neighborhood and since I had just lost mine—seemed like a good idea. From there, I don't remember a thing.

The next thing I knew, I was standing next to a state police officer on the side of the freeway. My mom's car was totaled. I was completely blacked out while driving and smashed into a wall. My head hit the steering wheel and I could have died or killed someone.

My blood alcohol level was .21, which was three times the legal limit in Michigan.

## A GLIMMER OF HOPE

I was arrested and taken to the local police station in one of the worst neighborhoods in Detroit. I don't even remember the ride, only sitting across a table from an officer with my mom on speakerphone trying to explain what happened. I was crying, I knew I messed up and this was the pinnacle of my trouble. Mom was hysterical that I just totaled her car understandably very angry. She told me I'd broken her trust and not to bother coming home. She added, that if I was still serious about getting better, I needed to check myself into Grace Centers of Hope, a faith-based treatment center. I agreed to do so, and I don't remember anything else from that night.

The next day I was taken to the hospital by police due to my injuries from the accident. I was handcuffed to the hospital bed to make sure I didn't escape. As I laid there, I noticed large chunks of blood on the curtain next to me. The nurse pointed to the bed and said the old man, that was in the bed had liver disease due to alcohol addiction. Hearing that scared me. I knew I was ready to change, but seeing that gave me all the motivation I needed.

I waited for several days in the local jail for my appearance before the judge. I knew I needed a miracle. I was already on probation in four different cities and had a restricted driver's license from my previous drinking and driving. As I sat in the bullpen with the other prisoners still feeling and reeking of alcohol, I prayed. I told God that if He would let me out with no bond, I would change my life and go to Grace Centers of Hope. I knew with my previous criminal record, it would take divine intervention for the judge to let me go free.

As I was called before the judge, my charge was read aloud. I pleaded not guilty. Believe it or not, the judge let me off with no bond. It was a MIRACLE and I knew I needed to hold up my end of my prayer to God. I called my Dad and asked him to take me to

## INTRODUCTION

the Grace Centers of Hope rescue mission. This was it for me—I needed a permanent change, starting now.

As we drove to the Center, I reflected on all of my decisions leading up to that point. I didn't want to be there, but I also didn't know how to get out of the web I entangled myself in and was ready for a positive change. I had tried before and even small stints in rehab programs, but they didn't work. I tried quitting drugs and alcohol numerous times, it never worked. This time needed to be different.

After saying goodbye to my Dad, I quickly realized I was the youngest person there—by far. I was surrounded by much older men hardened by years of living on the streets. The program was a year-long; was I going to last the year?

That night was rough. I was staying in a dorm of about 50-60 men. Old and dirty men struggling with issues just like me. We were all woken up with a bright light and told to head to chapel. Every day at the center started with a small church service devotional before breakfast. I shuffled along all the while asking myself how I ended up there.

That day, May 7th, 2002, a man and his family arrived at the Center. I didn't know it at the time, but God sent that man to me to help change my life. Dwayne was an older African American gentleman from the inner city. He had come to the center with his wife and kids seeking help due to his own struggles with addiction. He was a well-seasoned man of faith but had gotten off track and looked for help just like me.

I remember meeting him and instantly making a connection. He was very energetic and passionate. Dwayne eventually became a mentor to me and took me under his wing. He began to teach me about the Bible and would pray with me. He took the time to open up the scriptures with me and explained the importance of some of the stories in the Bible. It's like God was speaking directly to me through those pages.

One morning at Bible Study, I felt God speak to me for the first time. Not audibly, but in my spirit. He reminded me about my prayer that Cinco De Mayo Sunday morning. He heard me ask to experience church every day and answered immediately. I nearly began to weep. I was overwhelmed with that same feeling that I had at church that fateful morning before my car accident.

I felt alive and clean and I knew that despite how I got there, God was in control and knew that is where I would meet Dwayne, and more importantly, where I would meet Jesus. At the center, over the subsequent months, my life was radically changed. Jesus became real, the Bible made sense the more I read, and Dwayne and I became best friends. He taught me what it meant to follow Jesus. I would not be who I am today, or where I am in my life without Dwayne's friendship and example. He was my first mentor—and we are still friends today.

Through my time at the center, God prepared me for the road ahead. Although my life was changing and I was no longer drinking, doing drugs, or living a crazy lifestyle, I still needed to face the consequences of my actions. I had to go to court for the drunk driving case, as well as the related charges of violating probation in four other cities. By the looks of it, I was headed to jail—for a long time. I was nervous and Dwayne could see that. He prayed for me and shared a passage from the Bible and told me this verse helped him throughout life. This gave me peace and helped me remember to trust God.

*And we know that God causes all things to work together for good to those who love God, to those who are called according to His purpose. (Romans 8:28 NASB)*

## BOOT CAMP

As the judge called me forward for my sentencing for my second minor in possession of alcohol, I had peace in my heart. I had peace because I knew that I was truly a changed person and that God was in control and I trusted Him. The judge looked at my track record and sentenced me to 30 days in the Macomb County Jail. It was the last place I wanted to be, but I was blessed that it was only 30 days. I also knew this was only one of several other judges I'd have to soon stand in front of.

# INTRODUCTION

After serving 30 days, I went back to Grace Centers of Hope and began meeting with my probation officers. Believe it or not, I did not have to serve any other jail sentences as the probation officers recommended, I served the rest of my time at Grace Centers.

Although my time there was mostly positive, it was not without its trials and tribulations. I was still the young 19-year-old punk that ran his mouth. I always seemed to rub someone the wrong way. Many of the older guys, including the men's leader, did not like me. I was no longer on the streets and my life was changing for the better, but I was still young, immature, and carried a lot of baggage. One day I had got into an argument with the men's leader and was kicked out. I was supposed to be there 12 months as per the court order, so I knew that I was going to have to face another judge soon.

I left the center, got onto a bus, and headed back towards the area I used to live. As I sat on that hour-long bus ride, I reflected on the last several months. I was angry and frustrated at what happened at the center and felt a strong urge to drink and party again. Thankfully, God had changed me and given me the opportunity to witness others fall into relapse, a few of them, unfortunately, overdosed and even died. I knew that if I took a step in that direction again, that it could happen to me too, I wasn't willing to take that chance.

Not too long after leaving the Center, the men's leader had contacted one of my probation officers and provided her false information. He said the reason I was kicked out was that I threatened someone with a knife. It was plainly untrue, but there was not much I could do to defend myself. My probation officer told me she was going to violate me. I would be seeing the judge soon. He was not very happy. Neither was I.

My court date was set for my 20th birthday, Halloween 2002. My Mom and Grandma came with me to court. We prayed and put it in God's hands. Regardless of the outcome, I knew I was different. I was not the same person I was before; God had profoundly changed me. However, as the judge called me forward and began to read the notes given to him, I could see him visibly get angry, and for a moment I worried about my immediate future. Several months prior, this same Judge agreed to allow me to serve my sentence at Grace Centers. After reading the report from the probation officer and the testimony of the men's leader, I knew I was in trouble. He ripped into me. He told me I was no good for nothing and that I deserved the book to be thrown at me.

I heard my mom and grandma begin to cry in the seats behind me. The judge stood up, pointed at them, and shouted, "Don't you cry for him, he is nothing but trouble, and his life is a mess!" It was extremely difficult to hear, and even more to see him speak to my mom and grandma that way. He had no way of knowing about the real change in my life.

My sentence was to be six months in the county jail with work release, meaning they would allow me to go to work and return. The only problem was I did not have a job or a car. Earlier that day I heard someone mention something about a Boot Camp program. It was eight weeks long and one of the toughest programs in the country. Not everyone made it through and if you didn't you'd be back to the county jail to serve your entire sentence. I definitely wasn't ready to sit in a jail cell for six months, so I leaned over to my attorney and asked, "What about the Boot Camp program?" He asked the judge if I could do the Boot Camp program instead. The judge looked me straight in the eye and said, "You want Boot Camp, I'll give you Boot Camp," attempting to scare me I wasn't sure what to make of it.

I was handcuffed and escorted to the jail. They let me quickly turn to my mom and grandma to say goodbye. I didn't know what to expect, but I knew that if I completed the eight weeks, it would suspend the six-month sentence. Eight weeks didn't seem so bad, but boy was I in for a surprise. In the holding cell, one of the other inmates told me it could take months before there was an available spot in the Boot Camp program. This program was full, and they had two streams running at all times.

As I was getting fingerprinted and registered in the system, I felt peace and knew God was with me. I was not worried or fearful. I had been in this situation before, and I felt the different this time. The last time I was here was when I sold those fake drugs to the undercover cops. This time, I was a new man and knew that God

## INTRODUCTION

was with me. I learned about God's favor and blessings when I was at the center, and I had seen Him work in the courts with the judges. I was believing for the same here.

I remember one of the ladies getting me registered mentioning that a new boot camp group was scheduled to begin within the next few days. I believe that she was a Christian. We talked about the Lord and how my life had changed. At the moment I knew God was working on my behalf.

Later that night, after being moved to a gymnasium to sleep, I was told that I was accepted into the Boot Camp program. I was SO EXCITED that I did not have to wait several months! This was not how I expected to spend my 20th birthday, or that I'd be excited to go to Boot Camp. But I was. I had no way of knowing I was diving into the toughest experience of my life.

While waiting for Boot camp to start, several of the other inmates shared a few stories of what they had heard about the program. One of the guys was a repeat, as he didn't make it through the first time. I was told it was worse than Marine Corp Boot Camp and that all the instructors were former military sergeants. I knew this was going to be tougher than I originally imagined, but I was willing to go through it!

The big morning arrived. It was officially the start of the program and I was both equally nervous and excited. As we lined up, I saw 15 drill instructors dressed in army fatigue come burst through the doors. My heart sank. They were all yelling at the top of their lungs, pushing the inmates off the line and one by one yelling in their faces. It was worse than the movies. I knew my turn was coming so I mentally prepared myself.

The drill instructor approached me and tossed me against the wall. I tried to respond, and he barked back, "You don't talk unless I give you permission, you Maggot! And you address me as, Sir Yes Sir." He knew what I had been charged with and purposely began taunting me. "You think you are a tough drug dealer?!" he said, "You think you are the man? Well, for the next eight weeks you are going to be my little B*t@h!"…OMG. I was immediately rethinking this whole Boot camp thing. Six months of jail wasn't looking so bad now.

But, I wasn't just determined to make it through the program, I wanted to be a better man. So I was going to stick it out. That first day seemed so long but moved fast. There were no breaks, no time off, no time to even think. They brought us into the barracks and had us dress in full army fatigue. I was happy to take off the jail uniform. And just like you see in the movies, they shaved our heads and told us to stand at attention until given the next order. We stood for hours and my boots hurt my feet so badly. I was mentally, physically, and emotionally drained and it wasn't even noon.

We were not allowed to look the drill instructors in the eyes. If we did, we got yelled at and commanded to do push-ups. I think I did thousands of push-ups in those eight weeks. The ultimate goal was to break us down so they could then build us back up. We did not know it then and unfortunately many didn't even get that far.

We would often be woken up at 2:00 am, just after going to sleep at midnight to do physical training (PT). We were taken outside to bear crawl through the mud and do all sorts of crazy exercises. I remember being so tired one day I began to hallucinate. Several inmates broke down completely. When they did, the instructors forced them to wear a large yellow banana suit that had "quitter" written across the front. They would not allow you to just quit, they purposely shamed you. One guy intentionally went "crazy" so he could be taken back to jail.

It was an extremely difficult program, but I prayed daily that God would give me the strength I needed. As I progressed, I could feel myself becoming stronger and more disciplined. We were taught that you are only as strong as your weakest link. One morning, we had to do a seven-mile run. We were not allowed to walk. One of the inmates got tired and walked anyway. Because he walked, the rest of us were punished.

Many of the exercises, while incredibly tough, also brought us together as a team. The system the drill instructors used was the same as the military. The late nights, being woken up hours after falling asleep, carrying 100+ pound logs for hours, thousands of push-ups, running until we almost vomited (many actually would

## INTRODUCTION

vomit), lack of sleep, standing at attention, and the yelling—all of it—was part of a detailed plan. We were trainees on our way to being Cobras. There was even a graduation ceremony to look forward to.

Several weeks after being in the program, we witnessed the graduation of the platoon ahead of us. They received the title, "Cobra." I admired how accomplished they were and saw how their families beamed with pride. This eight-week experience was completely worth it. I began to be excited for the day I would graduate and make my family proud.

Soon after, another platoon of trainees joined us. The drill instructors relied on us, now the senior platoon, to show the juniors the ropes. Also, the drill instructors began putting us into leadership positions to test our skills. If the appointed platoon leader did not follow instructions or dropped the ball, they would be replaced.

At the graduation ceremony, we were also introduced to different awards and recognitions. The highest honor and recognition you could receive was the Distinguished Honor Graduate (DHG)—it was like being Valedictorian of leadership. I was determined to get that award. It was mine. Over the next several weeks I went above and beyond to serve and help my fellow trainees. When the drill instructors needed a volunteer, I stepped up.

The drill instructors took notice of my efforts. They put me in the position of platoon leader many times and tested me every opportunity they could. I did my best each and every day. I pushed through the pain, sleep deprivation, discouragement, and tests. While difficult, I thanked God for this opportunity, and for giving me a favor even here.

There was another trainee that also wanted to be the DHG. We ended up becoming good friends and worked hard together. We both wanted to be leaders, and we knew graduation was fast approaching. We told each other that no matter who received the award, we would celebrate and be happy for each other.

A few days before graduation, the drill instructors notified us they'd be choosing the DHG leader. I wanted this so badly, not only to prove this to myself but as evidence that I can truly do anything. The drill instructor walked into the hall to share the results—he said it had come down to two.

He said one, in particular, stood out, had gone above and beyond, and proven himself to be a leader of leaders. Then he said my name! I was the DHG! I had earned the highest possible ranking within the Boot Camp program. I felt so accomplished. I was so thankful to God; I knew He was with me and I had His favor. Receiving that award, I knew I could do anything!

As I reflected on the eight weeks, I truly felt like a new man! All the pain and hardship truly served their purpose. I was broken down and built back up. This was the greatest accomplishment of my life to date and I knew this was just the beginning.

The morning of our graduation was one of the greatest days of my life. My family came, and so did my mentor from Grace Centers, Dwayne, and his family. I could not wait for the ceremony to begin. I wanted to be named a Cobra. I walked into the ceremony so proud. I couldn't wait to see my family. Eight weeks had felt like an eternity.

When they called my name as the DHG, I could see the look on their faces. They were so happy—some even cried! This was my one and only graduation experience since I had dropped out of school, and it was awesome. The whole experience profoundly changed my life. It made me realize that if I could graduate with distinction from one of the toughest boot camp programs in the country, I could truly accomplish anything! (See my award on the following page.)

## INTRODUCTION

I acquired a level of physical, mental, and emotional discipline I did not know was possible. I learned how to work as a team and focus on others. The program was truly a success. I am glad I did not give up because I would have ultimately been giving up on myself. I left the grounds that day ready to take on the world!

# LET'S GO!

There are two things I know for sure; 1] every single individual has been created for a specific reason, and 2] life is hard, and you will face hardships at some point no matter how much you try and avoid them. Even now you are, most likely, either going into a trail, in the middle of a trail, or just coming out of a trail. God uses trials in our lives to build character in us. I will cover more of this later in the book.

You have no control over the circumstances of your birth, or the family you were born into. You might be wealthy, middle class or poor. You may have had life given to you on a golden platter or you may come from humble beginnings. You may come from a big family, a small family, or maybe you were an only child. It doesn't matter if your parents planned your conception, or you were an "accident," God created you for a purpose—and that's no accident. I'm glad you've picked up this book. Life isn't always easy, matter of fact, Life is Hard. Your life might be so difficult right now or you're not sure what your purpose here on earth is that you've decided to pick up this book. I'm so glad you did. Now, I'm going to share with you the **Seven Key Principles** on how you too can break free and breakthrough from the obstacles in your life and discover the reason God created you. I've shared my story—and it doesn't end there. I continue to apply these principles to overcome all challenges that I face even today.

What you have experienced in life and what you may be going through right now can either make you or break you. You have the power to choose! I want you to stop right now and make the decision that losing, and quitting are not an option! Regardless of what you have been through, what you are currently going through, and no matter what things you will face in the future, make the decision right now that YOU ARE GOING TO WIN!

I'm excited to walk you through the **Seven Key Principles** that changed my life and can change yours too!

# CHAPTER 1

# PRINCIPLE ONE – DISCOVERING YOUR PURPOSE

## Definition

***Purpose***—the reason for which something or someone exists or is created.

## Bible Verse

*"For I know the plans I have for you,"* declares the Lord,
*"plans to prosper you and not to harm you,
plans to give you hope and a future."*
(Jeremiah 29:11 NIV)

## Panning For Gold
A Story About Finding Your Purpose in Life
(Source: Better Life Coaching Blog, post July 19, 2013)

A frustrated young man went to see the wise man in his village. "I don't know what to do with my life. How do I find my purpose?" The young man asked. "Follow me," said the old man.

Silently, they trudged together to a faraway river where they found dozens of prospectors panning for gold.

"There are three types of prospectors here," the sage said. "What do you mean?" The young man inquired.

"There are those who strike gold straight away. Excited, they take their plunder, cash it in and live comfortably for the rest of their lives. Then there are those who pan for years. They know that there is gold here and they have seen others strike it rich, so they persist until they too find the gold that they've been searching for."

"What about the third type?" asked the young man.

"They are the individuals who get frustrated that they haven't found what they are looking for, so after a day, a week or a year or more, they give up, walk away and never find gold."

Slightly confused, the young man asked, "What has this got to do with finding my purpose?"

"Ah yes, the age-old question," the old man smiled and looked his companion in the eye. "There are those in life who look for their purpose and seem to find it almost immediately. From a young age, they have a clear sense of purpose and pursue their dreams with energy and enthusiasm. Some others have to look a bit harder, perhaps for many years, but if they persist and keep looking, they will find something to live for. Finally, there are those who want to know their purpose, but they become frustrated with the search and give up too soon, returning to a life of meaningless wandering."

"Can everyone find their purpose?"

"Is there gold in the river?" the wise man responded. "So, how do I find my own purpose?"

"Keep looking."

"But what if I want to find it quicker?"

"Son, there are no guarantees that you will be able to find it quickly, the only guarantee is that if you give up and stop looking for it, you'll never find it."

The young man looked despondent, feeling that he had wasted his time with the old man.

He felt a reassuring hand on his shoulder, "I can sense your frustration, but let me assure you, if you can find your true calling in life, you will live with passion, make the world a better place, be richer than you could imagine and feel as though the very face of God Himself is smiling upon you. That may happen next week, next year or in the years ahead, but the search will be worth it and your life will never be the same again. So for now, your purpose is to find your purpose."

"Thanks."

"Oh, and there's one other thing that I forgot to mention."
"What's that?"

"Just as those men and women need to get down to the river with a pan to find their gold, so we need to remain active to find our

# CHAPTER 1 PRINCIPLE ONE – DISCOVERING YOUR PURPOSE

purposes, we don't find it sitting around at home doing nothing."

It was getting late, so the two men turned for home and began their long walk back to the village.

As they walked, the young man was deep in thought about what he had just learned, and the wise man smiled to himself, knowing that conversations like this were an important part of living his own purpose.

Now, over to you.

Do you know your purpose for life? Are you still looking?

Or have you given up?

\*\*\*

At one point or another we've all asked ourselves, "What is my purpose," or "Why was I created?"

As human beings, we know deep down that there's more to life than our routines. There's more than just waking up each day, going to work, coming home, watching TV or talking on the phone, going to sleep, and doing it all over again. I remember a moment when I was about 15 years old. I sat on my porch one evening feeling really lost. I was looking at my life and did some soul searching. I asked myself, "What is the meaning of my life? Is this it? There has to be more to life than this?" As I write now, that moment is still so clear to me.

Maybe you can relate. Can you remember a time you've felt this way? Are you at this place now? If yes, I want you to know that you're moving in the right direction. Like the young man in the story observed, some find their purpose immediately while others take longer. I want to encourage you to find your purpose and the reason for which you've been born.

*"Discovering your purpose is the most significant thing you will do in your life, and you, your loved ones, and the world will be better off because you went on this journey."*
- Martin Kipp

Everyone's purpose is tied to one of two things: first, you'll make the world a better place (cliché, I know, but true nonetheless), or second, help people. Regardless of whether you create the latest technology, find a cure to cancer, or volunteer at a local charity, your purpose will fall into one of these two categories.

Discovering my purpose is one of the most important key principles that I've applied to my life. This discovery has transformed my life and helped me go from rock bottom as you heard in the beginning of this book to a full and purpose-filled life. I lived in a homeless shelter, addicted to drugs and alcohol after having dropped out of high school. Now, I am a successful entrepreneur, business owner, author, and motivational speaker. I'm a husband to my beautiful wife and best friend, Joy, and a dad to four amazing kids, Angelina, Emilio, Tiara, and Judah, one son-in-law Joel, also a grandpa to my first grandchild, Joel III.

Discovering my purpose gave me hope when I was going through the hardest of times of my life and still does even today. I first discovered my purpose when I was 19 years old. At the time I was living in the Grace Centers of Hope, a faith-based homeless shelter and rehabilitation center. It was there I began to hear others talking about the importance of discovering God's purpose for my life—and the importance of having a vision. At first, I truly had no idea what they meant, but I was curious enough to ask questions, after all, it sounded important. I felt like the young boy in the story above. Many of the older men at the Center seemed sure of their purpose and only made me want to find mine even more. Sometimes an individual can find their purpose immediately; it's possible. Mine was a process, as I'm sure yours will be too.

I believe God doesn't reveal your purpose all at once. He reveals it over time. I also believe that you discover more aspects and facets of your purpose as your vision and experience expand. The more you move forward, the clearer it becomes. I was told to be very intentional about discovering my purpose and the best way to do it was to find a quiet place, close my eyes, clear my mind to pray, and ask God to show me His purpose for my life. I was told to be ready with a pen and paper to jot down the first thing that came to mind. But truth be told, this was all very new to me, and besides, how would I know it was God speaking? I had so many questions like these, but I'd determined in my heart that I'd do whatever was necessary to discover it.

If you are a Christian, this may make sense to you, but if you're not and don't currently have a relationship with Jesus, then you might be reading this scratching your head and puzzled. That's okay—I've been there. The great thing is that no matter where you are at spiritually or wherever you are on your journey, my goal is that after reading this chapter (and the rest of this book!) that you learn the key principles I am going to give you to begin moving in the right direction and discover your purpose.

> *"For I know the plans I have for you," declares the Lord ,*
> *"plans to prosper you and not to harm you,*
> *plans to give you hope and a future."*
> (Jeremiah 29:11 NIV)

God has plans for your life. His plans are your purpose. What I love about the Bible verse above is that it's a promise that God has made and if you look at the definition of the word promise, it means 1] a declaration that one will do something specified and 2] a legally binding declaration that gives the person to whom it is made a right to expect or to claim it. So if God declares something like He does in Jeremiah 29:11 that means two things, 1] That it is legally binding, and God does not lie, and 2] you need to expect and claim that God has plans for your life and not just any plans, but plans to prosper you and not harm you, plans to give you hope and a future. You can literally take this one to the bank, because God has signed it, sealed it, and delivered it! So how do you figure out these plans God has for your life?

My pastor said something a few weeks ago I'd like to share with you. He said, "We don't create our own purpose in life because God has already created our purpose. Our job is to discover it." If there is any insecurity harboring inside you right now, rest in the fact that God created you and has plans for you. Ephesians 2:10 says, "*For we are his workmanship, created in Christ Jesus unto good works, which God hath before ordained that we should walk in them."* We are God's handiwork, created in Christ Jesus to do good works, which God prepared in advance for us to do." God has created you uniquely. You are the only "YOU" on the earth, and believe me when I say you have a divine mission only you can accomplish. You were created on purpose, for a purpose, and with a purpose.

God places specific desires in our hearts and those desires are often directly linked to our purpose. For example, perhaps you notice single moms around your neighborhood and think, "Someone should make a place for single women with kids to connect." Or perhaps as you pass the same homeless individual every day you think, "Someone should feed him. He looks hungry." Or maybe there's a failing program in your community center, workplace, or church, and you think, "We could help more people if someone would…" I'm sure you've already anticipated my next question, but what if that "someone" is you?

No circumstance or detail of your life is accidental. Where you live, when you were born, whom you've interacted with — God has placed them there, and He calls you to serve those around you. The best way to find your calling is to consider: Whom specifically are you burdened for? And, what opportunities has God provided to help these individuals? The answer to those questions will help you discover your purpose.

While some find a niche and dedicate their lives quickly, often the vast majority of individuals need to first grow through seasons and opportunities before their purpose is revealed. The desire to have a meaningful existence is innate in all of us. It's what motivates our late nights at the office or long days of school, our early morning practices, and other endeavors. We want to know that what we do matters, and that we are making a difference.

If you don't understand why you are here or what you were made for, the need will either be filled through expedience (i.e. we'll do whatever seems easy in the moment) or dissipation (i.e. the waste of time, money, and energy). The Bible teaches that searching for our purpose in anything or anyone other than Him will always leave us unfulfilled. For example, after observing all the ways people searched for meaning in their lives apart from

**CHAPTER 1 PRINCIPLE ONE – DISCOVERING YOUR PURPOSE**

God, King Solomon (the wisest and wealthiest person to ever live), wrote in Ecclesiastes 1:14, *"I have seen all the things that are done under the sun; all of them are meaningless, a chasing after the wind."* Only God has the answers you're looking for, and He promises that if you'll seek your purpose in Him, your life will have an eternal impact.

Best-selling, author, Jack Canfield puts it best, "You see, without a purpose in life, it's easy to get sidetracked on your life's journey. It's easy to wander and drift, accomplishing little. But with a purpose, everything in life seems to fall into place. To live "on purpose" means you're doing what you love to do, doing what you're good at, and accomplishing what's important to you. When you truly are living on purpose, the people, resources, and opportunities you need naturally gravitate toward you. The world benefits, too, because when you act in alignment with your true life purpose, all of your actions automatically serve others."

I am going to share with you the following steps that I used in helping me discover my purpose. I believe that if you apply these same steps, and make an effort to complete the exercises, you will discover yours as well.

Now, am I promising a perfect and concise plan after applying the following steps? No. There likely won't be. However, you will gain much more clarity and insight. This will create a much better environment for things to fall into place for you since you'll be in a position to recognize them.

Remember—it's a process. Resist the urge to grow impatient and frustrated and throw down your pan—you never know, your next batch might hit gold.

## Step 1: Discover Your Soul

The title sounds weird—but hear me out. From childhood, through no fault of our own, we've inherited the fears and limiting thoughts of the adults that surrounded us. We grew up conditioned to believe we may have limitations, and deep down we feared pursuing who we most want to be. As adults, we simply continued in these negative and restrictive mental environments. You need to identify, question and chip away at these mindsets. It's vital to recognize who we are on a soul level.

## Exercise

*Find a quiet place with no distractions and have a pen and paper handy. Ask yourself, "What would my life look like if I could do anything? If there were no limits—and the answer was always 'yes'—what would my day look like?" Write down everything that comes to mind, even the little details. Now, if you're like me and writing doesn't always flow, use a recording app on your phone or tablet. This might even be easier since you won't need to even open your eyes. Resist the urge to dive into a luxurious fantasy—I get it, we all want to chill on a beach in the Caribbean. Instead, focus on what lights a spark inside your heart.*

## Step 2: Discover Your Innate Abilities

Your purpose already exists. There's no stress for you in trying to build or make a purpose for yourself. Your job is to discover it, and who doesn't love a good adventure? In uncovering your purpose, you'll begin to shape and create the life you want. Of course, it takes work to develop your skill set—even the most gifted musicians still practice—but it should feel natural. The process should feel akin to rowing downstream rather than battling upstream. For example, I love to speak, sell, write, coach, train, and develop others. These things come easily to me. Although I've invested many years in honing these skills, I have loved every minute of it. Remember, work is required, but suffering is not. If you're struggling and suffering, you need to begin to question why and make changes to begin living on purpose.

## Exercise

*Same as in step 1, find a quiet place with a pen/paper or recording device. Ask yourself, "What am I good at? What comes easily to me? What talents do I have? What am I passionate about?" Again, write down everything that comes to* mind. *If you're having trouble, this is one of the only steps where you can get a trusted friend or family member involved. Sometimes it's hard to recognize or identify something that feels second nature.*

## Step 3: Discover Quietness

Learning to find and then live your purpose starts on the inside. Doing soul searching is difficult work. Delving deeply into your heart and mind can be exhausting, and finding a place to recharge. Ask any professional athlete, sleep and rest are critical to performance. Same with soul-work, schedule some purposeful quiet time.

## Exercise

*Go somewhere you can sit and relax without distraction, similar to the two previous exercises. Only this time, (you should be sure to have pen and paper just in case) your goal is to get out of your own head. Contemplate something bigger. Play relaxing music. Allow yourself to churn up and quietly mull over all you've considered in the past little while.*

## Step 4: Discover the Who and How

Once I was clean and sober, I discovered that I could use my gifts to communicate my journey. I felt so much compassion for those facing similar struggles to those I had been facing. Once I began to share about the change in my life, so many opportunities opened up for me to help others who were previously addicted to drugs and alcohol. My purpose at the time, and even the difficult moments in my life, began to take on a new light. I especially love sharing in schools with young people in hopes that I could perhaps steer them away from my previous mistakes.

## Exercise

*Is there an area of your life that you have struggled with where you can now help others? Sometimes the easiest place to begin is a misstep. Alternatively, is there a charitable organization or place nearby you've always wanted to volunteer at? If so, find a way to connect with the group or organization and get involved. Remember, it's impossible to steer a parked car—get moving and see what other opportunities present themselves.*

## Step 5: Discover The Bible (If you haven't already.)

Whether you're a Christian believer or not, the Bible is chocked-full of wisdom and insight. One of the simplest ways to discover your purpose is to go straight to the source. The Bible is not a regular book or a dead letter. It's alive and speaks just as profoundly to us modern folks as it does to the ancients. Trust me on this one.

## Exercise

*If you don't have a Bible, purchase one or download the app called "You Version." If you already have one, open it up. Start with reading 15-20 minutes a day. I recommend you start reading the Gospel of John in the New Testament. You'll want to have with you something to write down the verses that really pop out.*

## Step 6: Spend Time With God

Depending on your experience, this may sound odd or like a no-brainer. But let me tell you in no uncertain words—you can and want to hear from God. Life, the hustle and bustle and distraction of it, drowns out His voice. Do me a favor and begin to implement this in your day-to-day life. Shut off the TV, put your phone on silent, step away from the laptop and focus on Him. Psalm 46:10 says, "Be still, and know that I am God."

## Exercise

*Take everything you have written down for steps 1 through 6 and ask God to speak to you. Ask Him flat-out to reveal His purpose to you. I love to pray and spend time with God before my day gets started, but you can pray anytime. If you've got some free time after lunch or in the evening, start small and weed out the clutter in your daily routine. If you commute to work, turn off the music and pray or listen to scripture while driving (or riding). Even five or ten minutes of prayer and reading the Bible can make a difference—and you may find that He's been trying to speak purpose into your life all along.*

## Step 7: Take Inspired Action

It's time to take action (if you haven't already). You don't need, at this point, a fully developed and linear plan to follow. Decide daily, or even moment-to-moment what you will do next. The point is to relentlessly pursue your passions with the intention of discovering your purpose. Take note of opportunities that come your way and act on those that resonate.

## Exercise

*Ask yourself every morning (until it becomes second nature), "What action will I take today in pursuit of my purpose?" Then go do it. Live on purpose.*

## Prayer

*God, thank You for allowing me to be born into this world and be alive at this very place in history. Lord, help me to discover my purpose and the reason why You created me. Give me ears to hear and eyes to see what You have called me to do in Jesus' Name, Amen!*

# CHAPTER 2

# PRINCIPLE 2 – CREATE A VISION

## Definition

***Vision***—Something seen in a dream; a thought, concept, or object formed by the imagination; manifestation to the senses of something immaterial; the act or power of imagination; mode of seeing or conceiving; unusual discernment or foresight; the act or power of seeing.

## Bible Verse

*"Where there is no vision, the people perish."*
(Proverbs 29:18)

## Three Fish and the Fisherman
(Source: FitPro Essentials, posted in Tips, July 23, 2020)

Once upon a time, there lived three fish in a pond. One was named "Plan Ahead," another was "Think Fast," and the third was called "Wait and See."

One day they heard a fisherman say that he was going to cast his net in their pond the next day.

Plan Ahead said, "I'm swimming down the river tonight!" and so he did.

Think Fast said, "I'm sure I'll come up with a plan."

Wait and See lazily said, "I just can't think about it now!" When the fisherman cast his net the following morning, Plan

Ahead was long gone.

But Think Fast and Wait and See were caught!

Think Fast quickly rolled his belly up and pretended to be dead. "Oh, this fish is no good!" said the fisherman and threw him safely back into the water.

Wait and See ended up in the fish market.

\*\*\*

**UNLEASHED**, by Justin Ford

Whom do you relate to the most? Which fish are you? As Jonathan Swift, the 18th-century Irish author, said, "Vision is the art of seeing what is invisible to others." Plan Ahead was able to see something that, "Think Fast and Wait and See" could not. This chapter is designed to help you create a vision for your future, no matter which fish you identify with the most. You can't arrive at a destination without first knowing where you're going. We are going to dive into what your endgame looks like. In the previous chapter, we covered the importance of discovering your purpose. My Pastor, Apostle Ellis Smith, says, "Discovering your purpose comes before vision because purpose speaks to why you exist, your reason for being. When you know your purpose, it energizes you. The vision reveals what you are supposed to be doing with your life and how it is supposed to look. If you do not discover your purpose first, you will lack the drive to carry out your vision when life brings difficult challenges." Purpose and Vision function like hand-in-glove. One without the other leaves both incomplete. Once you've discovered your purpose, creating a vision will help you get there.

One of my mentors, Christopher John, founder of the Empowerment Center, describes vision this way:

> "A vision is an experience that appears vividly or credibly to the mind, although not currently present in your physical experience. Visioning allows you to focus your awareness on things you desire, even when you have not achieved, acquired, or experienced them. Visioning can become a very powerful practice when you use it to discover your greatest desires, commitments, goals, and missions in life."

## CHAPTER 2 PRINCIPLE TWO – CREATE A VISION

*The only thing worse than being blind is having sight but no vision.*

- Helen Keller

The above quote is from a truly remarkable woman. Helen Keller contracted a rare illness when she was just 19 months old. It left her blind and deaf for the rest of her life. Even though she could communicate her basic needs by signing to relatives, her life was very difficult and with little hope. With the help of her teacher, Anne Sullivan, Keller went on to graduate with a Bachelor of Arts degree and become a prolific American author.

Your vision is your most crucial mental picture or dream. It can also be a set of long-term goals. A vision defines your optimal desired future state; it tells of what you would like to achieve over a longer time. It's the road map to fulfilling your purpose. You have the potential to change your world—your surroundings—in a very fundamental way. Do not be afraid to project yourself and your vision onto the world.

*Think about this…everything first started with a VISION!*

You first need to visualize something before you can create it. Every invention you see in the material world was first visualized. For example, the Wright brothers had a vision of flight. They had a vision of safe and efficient air travel. They imagined what that kind of air vehicle would look like and got started. Henry Ford had a vision of millions of people using automobiles before creating the assembly line and making it possible. Bill Gates, the founder of Microsoft, envisioned a desktop computer in every home before the first was successfully constructed.

One of my favorite examples of visualization is from the comedian Jim Carey. He wasn't always wealthy and famous. For a long time, Carey was broke and struggled for a future in entertainment. He appeared on the Oprah Show in 1997 and told a fantastic story. One night he wrote himself a check for $10 million dollars for "acting service rendered" and dated it for Thanksgiving, 1995. He carried it in his wallet for years and would look at it every morning and every night. Then, just before Thanksgiving 1995, Carey received the news that he would earn $10 million dollars for his role in "Dumb and Dumber."

That's the power to visualize your dreams and relentlessly believe and work toward your vision every day. Everything first starts with VISION! You must first see it to believe it in order to achieve it.

> *Have a vision. It is the ability to see the invisible. If you can see the invisible you can achieve the impossible.*
> 
> *- Shiv Khera*

I grew up with the mindset of the fish "Wait and See." I believe that not understanding or having a vision for my future led me to all the hardship and trouble I experienced early on. I lived in the moment with no purpose and no vision. I made lots of bad decisions that nearly took my life. While those times were rough, they ultimately led me to discover my purpose and create a vision for my life.

In the first section of this book, I go over my story and how at 19 years old, I was living in a homeless shelter. It wasn't easy. Many of the other men were much older than me, and some passed away from their substance abuse issues during my stay. I witnessed first-hand how their lifestyle choices made their day-to-day life unbearable. I knew that wasn't what I wanted for myself but didn't know how to change it. Thankfully, Dwayne was able to look past my smart mouth and know-it-all attitude that often got me into trouble. As I mentioned, he took me under his wing and spoke to me about having a purpose, reading the Bible, and having a vision for my future.

Even though my prospects did not look great living in a homeless shelter, I finally began to see and develop a vision and bright future for my life. At night, when everything was quiet, I would pray and ask God to give me a vision and show me what my future would be. I would close my eyes and see myself married to a beautiful Christian woman. (Not just any Christian woman, I remember writing down specifically that I wanted an exotic wife with brown skin. When you write down your vision, you want to list the details precisely. Lo and behold I married Joy, who is Mexican and Filipino with beautiful brown skin…lol.) With

## CHAPTER 2 PRINCIPLE TWO – CREATE A VISION

lots of kids and living for God together. I saw us as successful partners in business, living well, traveling far, and enjoying life! Compared to the reality of the circumstances at the time, it seemed impossible or unlikely, but I was living too much in that vision to ever give room to doubts. As God began to reveal my future, I began to understand that THIS IS VISION—the ability to imagine and picture something that is not your current reality but what it can be.

A vision for your life is more than just a to-do list; it is a proclamation of the outcome of your life. The purposeful intention of what you aim to accomplish during the days you walk on this earth. A vision is knowing your goal and destination without knowing the inevitable detours along the way. It is similar to using a GPS traveling to a destination you have never been to before. You plug in the address, the GPS calculates the best route from your current location, and there is an estimated arrival time. Having a vision is very similar. Think of your vision as the light shining in the darkness that illuminates your life path. Vision does not eliminate distractions or obstacles. It inspires us to focus on what matters. Vision provides clarity for the future while directing us to focus on the present.

I think one of the greatest gifts God ever gave to man is not the gift of sight, but the gift of vision.

> *Sight is a function of the eyes, but vision is a function of the heart.*
> 
> - Myles Munroe

Having a vision is so vital that even the Bible says, in Proverbs 29:18, "*Where there is no vision, the people perish.*" What a compelling and bold statement! The definition of perish—look it up—literally means to disappear or suffer destruction or ruin.

So, if vision fuels our mental picture to pursue our life's purpose, what does not having a vision look like? Well…just have a close look at the world today and the immense problems we face. For example, murder, hate crimes, racism, division, extreme poverty, injustice, and gross immorality, to name a few. The list sadly goes awfully long. Another question? Do you think we would still have all these problems if every human being decided to discover their purpose and had a vision for their lives? I firmly believe one of the reasons we have all these problems stems from people not having any vision. Remember—where there is no vision, people perish (i.e., disappear in destruction and ruin).

Maybe you can relate to what I am saying. Perhaps you can see how not having a vision has caused a lot of wasted time and roaming in your own life. Are you experiencing some type of disappearance, destruction, or ruin currently? The good news is there is hope! Your life can change. You can experience a better way. I know you can because I have. So let me show you exactly how to get started!

There is another verse in the Bible that speaks precisely on what to do with a vision. In Habakkuk 2:2, God says to Habakkuk (a prophet—i.e., someone who hears directly from God), *"Write down the vision and make it plain on tablets, that he may run who reads it."* In this case, God was asking Habakkuk to write the vision so large on the stone that someone running past could still read it. That is not what I'm asking you to do. Instead, I just need you to write it down. Writing the vision is in obedience to what God has asked us to do, and that simple act shifts us from passive to active and engaged go-getter. Writing the vision down starts bringing it to life and clearing the path for progress. Be warned—If you don't write the vision down, you will likely forget it. It is not enough for it to be a daydream. You need a clear Vision Statement and Plan for your life. Hang it in a place you will see it every day—read it out loud (more than once!)—allow it to become second nature to you. Your vision needs to become so real to you that it is as if you're already there!

Now, let's get into the nitty-gritty of it. A good Vision Plan is made up of two parts—Statement and Plan.

The "Statement" ideally should be short, simple, and specific to you. Second, the "Plan" should be more specific and contain ambitions and goals. Goals are simply individual experiences and accomplishments that you strive for. Your "Vision Statement" is the big picture. Your vision plan will define who you want to be, what you want to be known for, and the set of experiences and accomplishments you aim for. It will help you define your goals and provide a framework for evaluation.

Your vision becomes your why. It can help light your path in seasons or moments of darkness and inspire us to shed or let go of anything holding you back.

In his best-selling classic, "7 Habits of Highly Effective People," Steven Covey, an American author and businessman, encouraged his readers to "Begin with the end in mind."

Your Vision Plan should aim to answer questions like:

What life do you want to have lived at age 20, 30, 40, 50, 60, 70 and 80?

What kinds of people do you want to be surrounded by?

What do you believe you are capable of in life? What are the most significant things you could accomplish, given the right circumstances, resources and motivation?

What do you wish you could change about the world? What could you contribute to the world that would make you feel proud and content?

What would you want people to say and remember about you when you die?

Your Vision Statement can be a sentence or two, or your vision statement can be a page long.

For example, Oprah Winfrey's vision is:

*"To be a teacher. And to be known for inspiring my students to be more than they thought they could be."*

And Richard Branson's vision is:

*"To have fun in [my] journey through life and learn from [my] mistakes."*

Here is a sample template of a long-form vision statement (to give you some ideas if you're stuck):

I will live each day as though I had all the power and influence necessary to make it a perfect world. Through listening to and serving others, I will learn new ideas and gain different perspectives. I will strive to gain mastery over life's challenges by increasing my circle of influence and deemphasizing those areas of concern I have no control over. I will behave in a manner to become a light, not a roadblock, for others who choose to follow or lead me. I will trust my dreams and be the prisoner of nothing. I will use my private victories unselfishly by creating value for others. The pursuit of excellence will determine the options I decide to exercise and the paths I choose to travel. I will expect no more of others than I expect of myself. I will seek new sources for learning and growth—nature, family, literature, new acquaintances. I will show love rather than expect love. I choose to focus on being effective versus efficient. I choose to make a difference in this world. You want to allow your vision to paint a mental picture of your life five to 20 years from now. Have it highlight what matters most to you, what you stand for, and who you are committed to becoming. Write it in the present tense so that it feels as if it exists right now.

Hopefully, you are starting to see not only the importance of having a vision for your life but that it is necessary. I want you to keep in mind that creating a vision is not something you want to force; you want to let it come to you naturally and gradually. Nearly 20 years after being in that homeless shelter, I live the life that I envisioned as a young, freshly off-the streets 19-year-old. I ended up marrying that amazing Christian woman 16 years ago. We have four exceptional children, live in an affluent neighborhood, drive nice cars, make an excellent income, own multiple businesses, travel on a regular basis, but most importantly, God is using us to help others and build His Kingdom precisely the way I envisioned it. So, I want you to know that THIS WORKS!!

Next, I am going to give you some steps on how to get started in creating a vision board.

## CHAPTER 2 PRINCIPLE TWO – CREATE A VISION

# Exercise: Create a Vision Board

Once you have written your vision statement, make sure to read it daily and create a vision board that aligns visually. A vision board is a tool used to help you concentrate and maintain focus on specific life goals. I find that physically seeing my vision written and displayed empowers and reminds me to walk in it every day. It reminds you of what is possible and keeps you focused when you are hit with a detour or some discouragement.

1. Go through your magazines (or favorite blogs or Google search) and tear/print the images. No gluing or pinning yet! Just let yourself have lots of fun looking through magazines and pulling out pictures or words or headlines that strike your fancy. Have fun with it. Make a big pile.
2. Go through the cutouts and begin to lay your favorites on the board. Eliminate any images that no longer feel right—be ruthless. This step is where your intuition comes in. As you lay the pictures on the board, you'll get a sense of how the board should be laid out. For instance, you might assign a theme to each corner of the board. Health, Job, Spirituality, Relationships, for example. Or it may just be that the images want to go all over the place. *I strongly recommend that this board be physical—not digital. You can have a picture or copy on Pinterest or another app or file on your phone, but the board should be physical. Head over to a nearby dollar store for some Bristol board or a corkboard—it doesn't need to be expensive.
3. Glue/pin everything onto the board. Add writing if you want, and you can even put a date on it of when you hope for each thing to become a reality. Or paint a section.
4. (Optional, but powerful and recommended) Leave space in the very center of the vision board for a fantastic photo of yourself where you look radiant and happy. Paste yourself in the center of your board.
5. Hang your vision board in a place where you will see it often. If you share a room or don't have a place that's just your own, consider making it foldable (like a book) and placing it in a shoe box or somewhere that's secret and special to you. Visit it often.

## Bonus Exercise for Single People:

    Remember how I told you that I wrote down I wanted an exotic wife with brown skin? Well, that was not the only thing I wrote down what I wanted in a wife. Back in 2005, I was at an Amway business conference, and I remember one of the speakers telling the story of how she found the husband of her dreams and that he was exactly what she had envisioned. She addressed the single people in the audience and told us exactly what to do to find the spouse of our dreams. She began to share an exercise with us that she also followed in order to find her husband. She said, when you get home, I want you to close your eyes and envision your dream spouse. What do they look like, what color is their hair, what type of body features do they have, what kind of personality do you want them to have? She said to get as detailed as possible, write down the vision, and make it plain. I was so excited to get home and begin this exercise. I was so ready to find my wife and get married. I was 22 and single and had just gained full custody of my daughter Angelina and because her mom was not involved in her life, I was also ready to find Angelina another mom.

    When I got home, one of the first things I did was sit down and begin to write my list of my future wife. As instructed, I listed as many details as possible. I wanted a wife with similar goals and dreams, travel and be in business together, be a great mom to Angelina, and yes, I wanted a beautiful brown-skinned exotic woman. But most importantly, I wanted a wife that loved Jesus. Hey, there is nothing wrong with wanting the absolute best! As I wrote my list, I could literally feel butterflies of excitement in my stomach at the thought of one day finding my bride. After finishing, I prayed over it and asked God to prepare me to be the man that would one day be the husband to this beautiful woman I had envisioned. After praying, I folded it up and put it in a shoe box in my closet.

    Before writing my list, I sized up every girl I met to see if they were my future wife. I was growing discouraged because I was not clear on what I wanted and so I would always find one or two things that I did not like, so I kept looking. It was not until writing my vision of a future wife down that I knew exactly what I wanted, and therefore I no longer needed to size up every girl because I knew what I was looking for. The great thing about knowing exactly what you want is that you can decide that you will not settle for second best.

One month later, I met Joy, and she literally checked off ALL the boxes on the list I wrote of my future wife. Because I knew what I wanted, I did not have to second guess it, and within eight months of meeting, we were married on December 3rd, 2005. At the time of writing this book, we just celebrated our 15th anniversary.

If you are single, I want you to do the same thing I did. I want you to get to a place, close your eyes, and envision the qualities, characteristics, and features you want in a spouse. Get as detailed as possible, then I want you to write it down, pray over it, and never settle for second best. I promise you once you know what you want, write it down and make the vision plain, and commit it over to God. Then in His timing, you will eventually meet your future spouse, and you will know it right away. This is how you develop a vision for your future spouse.

## PRAYER

*God, please help me to create a "Vision" for my life. Reveal specific details of the things You have called me to do and I also pray that I would discover Your very best for me in all areas of my life in Jesus' Name, Amen!*

# CHAPTER 3

# PRINCIPLE 3 - FORGIVENESS

## Definition

***Forgiveness***—the action or process of forgiving or being forgiven. It is a conscious, deliberate decision to release feelings of resentment or vengeance toward yourself, a person or group who has harmed you, regardless of whether they deserve your forgiveness. Forgiveness is not forgetting, nor does it mean condoning or excusing offenses.

## Bible Verse

*"Let all bitterness and wrath and anger and clamor and slander be put away from you, along with all malice. Be kind to one another, tender-hearted, forgiving each other, just as God in Christ also has forgiven you."*
(Ephesians 4:31-32 NASB)

## A Mother Forgives
(Source: Madamsabi's Blog, post June 4th 2015, as reported by The Forgiveness Project)

In June 1973, Marietta Jaeger went camping in Badlands National Park with her husband, Bill, and their five children. As they slept in their tents one night, their seven-year-old daughter, Susie, was kidnapped. Marietta suffered all the pain and emotional turmoil you would expect in such a nightmarish situation. In the days immediately following the abduction, she was surrounded by people who talked about the kidnapper in venomous terms, routinely characterizing him as inhuman (even though his identity and gender were still a mystery).

Despite this climate of anger and vengeance, something inside Marietta began to shift as the days of waiting turned into weeks. As reported in the May/June 1998 issue of Health Magazine, Marietta heard a voice.

"What Marietta heard was God telling her, 'I don't want you to feel this way.' As she pondered the message, the weight on her chest seemed to lift and her stomach relaxed. She fell into the first deep sleep since Susie vanished." This was the beginning of her commitment to releasing her anger and finding a path to forgiveness.

One year after the abduction the kidnapper called Marietta's home. Because she had used the intervening months praying for forgiveness—searching within for the strength to find the humanity buried somewhere within the kidnapper—she was able to convey genuine empathy as she spoke with him. Despite the obvious risks to the kidnapper, Marietta kept him on the phone for more than an hour, ultimately providing the FBI with enough information to locate and capture him. His name was David Meirhofer. He had abducted and killed other children. In FBI custody, he confessed to murdering Susie Jaeger a week after taking her from the family's tent. A few hours later, he committed suicide.

Given Meirhofer's horrific revelation, it would be understandable for Marietta to abandon the course of forgiveness. Her husband never let go of his anger and he died of a heart attack at 56 after suffering for years with bleeding ulcers, but Marietta stayed the course. She began traveling around the country to speak with others about forgiveness, sharing her experience. She even befriended the kidnapper's mother, Eleanor Huckert. "She and Huckert went together to visit the graves of their children," the Health article concludes. "Afterward, the two mothers sat at the Huckert's dining room table sipping coffee and thumbing through old scrapbooks. There was David on the front porch—a rosy-cheeked little boy, scrubbed and eager to set out for his first day of school. As she studied the smiling boy in the snapshot, Marietta felt that her struggle to invest the faceless criminal with humanity was complete. 'If you remain vindictive, you give the offender another victim,' she says. 'Anger, hatred, and resentment would have taken my life as surely as Susie's life was taken.'"

*\*\**

## CHAPTER 3 PRINCIPLE THREE - FORGIVENESS

Most people carry bitterness and unforgiveness in their hearts. They do not even realize it. At some point in our lives, we have all been hurt, wronged, let down, or taken advantage of by others. Some like Marietta have been wounded so badly that it feels impossible to forgive.

But unforgiveness—sometimes—is worse than the offense. Unforgiveness is like a disease that slowly destroys you on the inside. It begins to control how you feel and act. Have you ever met someone who was always angry? Someone who always must defend themselves, even when no one's confronting them? Many times, the underlying issue is unresolved pain from unforgiveness. You may be reading this thinking—Justin, you just do not understand how badly I've been wronged—you'll never understand my pain. You may be right. But I do know the effects of having bitterness and unforgiveness in my heart for years.

Being fully honest, forgiving someone who offended you or harmed you is not easy. If it were, you would have done it a long time ago. For example, I cannot imagine the pain and suffering that Marietta went through after her daughter was kidnapped and killed. Yet, she chose to forgive her offender. Forgiveness is a choice at the root, and she decided to allow God to transform her heart and forgive. Now please understand when I say I am not trying to minimize your pain, but if Marietta found a way to forgive—you can too.

> *"When you hold resentment toward another, you are bound to that person or condition by an emotional link that is stronger than steel. Forgiveness is the only way to dissolve that link and get free."*
>
> - Catherine Ponder

Some hurt run so deep it seems impossible to forgive. You may have been hurt, abandoned, or neglected at some point in your life. The pain and unforgiveness from those moments and events weigh so heavily they keep you from moving forward. You cannot seem to enjoy life; you can't seem to search out meaning or purpose.

The root issue is a low-boiling rage or numbness on the inside. Everything offends you like a raw live-wire, or nothing registers like a hard stone. These are the chains of offense and unforgiveness—recognize them for what they are.

Unforgiveness creates an invisible prison around the victim of the offense. Some carry the unforgiveness for many years. We see this with Marietta's husband, Bill. He chose to remain bitter and eventually suffered bleeding ulcers, a heart attack, and died. Now, I am not saying there weren't other contributing medical factors. However, there's clear evidence that links unforgiveness to a myriad of health issues. Here is what John Hopkins School of Medicine has to say about the effects of unforgiveness and your health:

> "Whether it's a simple spat with your spouse or long-held resentment toward a family member or friend, unresolved conflict can go deeper than you may realize—it may be affecting your physical health. The good news: Studies have found that the act of forgiveness can reap huge rewards for your health, lowering the risk of heart attack; improving cholesterol levels and sleep; and reducing pain, blood pressure, and levels of anxiety, depression, and stress. And research points to an increase in the forgiveness-health connection as you age. "There is an enormous physical burden to being hurt and disappointed," says Karen Swartz, M.D., director of the Mood Disorders Adult Consultation Clinic at The Johns Hopkins Hospital. Chronic anger puts you into a fight-or-flight mode, which results in numerous changes in heart rate, blood pressure, and immune response. Those changes, then, increase the risk of depression, heart disease, and diabetes, among other conditions. Forgiveness, however, calms stress levels, leading to improved health."

Wow! It is both scary and amazing to know how the body's systems respond to negative emotions. Releasing those emotions is not only good for your mental wellbeing but apparently for your immune system too. It is also a must if you want to move forward and experience the life God has destined for you.

I carried unforgiveness for many years. I was young and did not recognize it for what it was. My parents divorced when I was two years old. I do not have any vivid memories, but my dad's absence caused pain. My mom told me a story about one time when my dad was scheduled to pick me up one day so we could spend the weekend together. My bag was packed, my jacket on, and I stood waiting at the window. I was so excited—but he never showed. Mom said I was inconsolable once I understood he was not coming. I vaguely remember it.

This was followed by so much more. My mom remarried shortly after she divorced my dad. I lived with her and my stepdad for ten years until they, too, divorced. My mom moved out to live with her boyfriend before the divorce was final. It truly tore our family apart—literally. As mentioned earlier in the book, I went to live with my dad, one sister went to live with my mom, and my other sister stayed with my stepdad. My step-sister went to live with her aunt. Overnight the family was scattered. I was twelve, and it was too hard emotionally to deal with. I blamed my mom; it created a lot of bitterness.

In my mind, the silver lining of the situation was that I got to live with my dad. I always secretly wanted to live with him. I stayed with my dad for six years until I was 18. He was tough on me. Sometimes he'd get explosively angry and even physical. I eventually became bitter towards him as well. I was unaware at the time of just how much pent-up pain and bitterness I carried. The unforgiveness and blame I held against my parents, I now believe, was a major contributing factor to my poor decisions. I ran right into substance abuse, sexual activity, and toxic relationships. I was looking for approval and fulfillment in all the wrong places.

## SETTING MYSELF FREE FROM UNFORGIVENESS

It was not until my early twenties, after I became a Christian, that I truly realized the pain and unforgiveness that I was still carrying. Bitterness and unforgiveness towards my parents would sometimes spill over whenever they would speak. At the time, I did not know where this frustration was coming from, but it would trigger something within me and cause me to respond in a negative way.

I knew that at some point, I was going to need to let this out or address it constructively, but I had no idea how. For many years I held back my anger towards my dad. I was afraid he would get physical or cut the relationship. One day, sadly, he said something over the phone that ultimately triggered me. I flew off the handle and let out years of pent-up hurt. It was ugly. I said a lot of mean things, but at the moment, I did not care how it was going to be received. As I finished my tirade, his response caught me completely off guard. He was quiet for a few moments and then almost whispered, "Son, I never knew you felt that way. I'm so sorry." I was shocked.

I was completely jaw-on-the-floor shocked! I was sure his response would have been a mirror of my own, but I was wrong.

The situation was similar with my mom. When she left to live with her new boyfriend, I was livid. Divorce is an ugly and painful thing. When you are a kid, you can't possibly understand all the factors involved, and all you experience is pain. Unfortunately, we carry lots of those experiences and emotions into our adult lives, and it inevitably affects our relationships.

Reliving the wrong that was done to us keeps us living in the past. It also steals from us the opportunity to live right now. Forgiveness frees us to live in the present and ultimately benefits our growth and happiness.

Forgiveness allows us to move on without anger, contempt or seeking revenge. It lets us regain our personal agency. Our anger, regret, hatred, or resentment towards someone means that we give up our power and self-control. Envision a chain around your neck, controlled by the one who wronged you. Until you can forgive, you are their captive.

Forgiveness also clears the cobwebs so that you can see the good again. When you forgive, you will see all the positive qualities in the person who hurt you. And yes, contrary to what you may believe, they are there.

Maybe the unforgiveness you carry isn't towards your parents, perhaps you were bullied as a child, or you're being bullied now. Or perhaps someone took advantage of you, or you were sexually assaulted.

## CHAPTER 3 PRINCIPLE THREE - FORGIVENESS

Many things can cause unforgiveness, but in order to move forward, we must choose to forgive. So how do we do that?

## Exercise

I want you to sit down and list all of the people who have hurt you or taken advantage of you. Maybe you have been carrying unforgiveness for so many years that you have almost forgotten. I want you to write the names of the individuals and their offenses towards you. I want you to close your eyes, relive that moment or moments, feel the pain and now look that person in the eyes (even it is only in your imagination) and say, "You can't hurt me anymore." Now, I want you to forgive them. This may be an exceedingly difficult exercise, but this exercise is absolutely necessary to move past the pain.

After you have done this exercise, if you really are brave enough, I want you to reach out to that person and tell them that you forgave them for the pain they caused you. Do not be surprised if they didn't even know that you felt that way like my dad. If doing that is not possible, because maybe they passed away or can't reach out to them in person, release forgiveness in your heart towards them.

## Prayer

*God, forgive me for carrying bitterness and unforgiveness in my heart. Help me to forgive those who have hurt me and bring healing into my life in Jesus' Name, Amen!*

# CHAPTER 4

## PRINCIPLE 4 – FREEDOM FROM FEAR

### Definition

*Fear* - emotion induced by perceived danger or threat, which causes physiological changes and ultimately behavioral changes, such as fleeing, hiding, or freezing from perceived traumatic events.

### Bible Verse

*"I prayed to the Lord, and He answered me; He freed me from all my fears."*
(Psalm 34:4 GNT)

### Dope on a Rope
(Source: notsalmon.com,
as quoted in "How to be Happy Dammit")

There once was this criminal who had committed a crime. (Because, hey, that's what criminals do. That's their job!)

Anyway, he was sent to the king for his punishment. The king told him he had a choice of two punishments. He could be hung by a rope, or take what's behind the big, dark, scary, and mysterious iron door.

The criminal quickly decided on the rope.

As the noose was being slipped on him, he turned to the king and asked:

"By the way, out of curiosity, what's behind that door?"

The king laughed and said:

"You know, it's funny, I offer everyone the same choice, and nearly everyone picks the rope."

"So," said the criminal, "Tell me. What's behind the door? I mean, obviously, I won't tell anyone," he said, pointing to the noose around his neck.

The king paused then answered:

"Freedom. It seems most people are so afraid of the unknown, they immediately take the rope."

***

What intense emotions fear stirs up! So many people worldwide struggle daily with some type of fear. What I have personally learned from anxiety over the years is simply this… it's a BIG FAT LIAR. But we'll get to that later.

At its root, "*fear* is a worldly emotion triggered by the thought of losing something" (source unknown). It is true. Pause and think about it for a moment. Whether it is afraid to fly, because of the fear of crashing, or the fear of public speaking, because of exposure or vulnerability, fear has the potential to limit all kinds of events and opportunities in your life—if you let it. Regardless of the fear you struggle with, fear is a bully in your life, and until you learn how to overcome it, you will stay stuck and never experience freedom on the other side.

Here are the top ten fears people reported the most:

- FEAR OF FLYING: Flying is statistically the safest form of travel, yet this fear is rated at number #1. Honestly, if you have made it to the airport unharmed, you've already made it through the most dangerous part of air travel.
- FEAR OF PUBLIC SPEAKING: This ranks higher than the fear of death, meaning, at a funeral, individuals would prefer being in the coffin than being the one giving the eulogy.
- FEAR OF HEIGHTS: At its root, this is the fear of falling, and the higher you are, the "higher" the likelihood of losing balance, etc.
- FEAR OF THE DARK: This fear typically stems from childhood. Overcoming the fear of darkness begins with answering one question, "What do you think is in the darkness that can harm you?"
- FEAR OF INTIMACY: This is closely linked to the fear of rejection. They are often interlinked.

- FEAR OF DEATH: It also extends to anything death-related. (If you struggle here, I recommend reading 1 Corinthians 15:26. It may open your eyes to what—or better whom—death really is. Then consult 1 Thessalonians 4:13-18. (Spoiler alert! Death is not the "scary" end it professes to be).
- FEAR OF FAILURE: this manifests itself in different ways, most commonly through procrastination.
- FEAR OF REJECTION: at its root, this fear places your worth and power into the hands of another human being. You need to be convinced of your own value and worth—this is misplaced, fundamentally misplaced faith.
- FEAR OF SPIDERS: Spiders are so small. Most of us live in areas where we do not encounter big ones or poisonous ones on the daily. As far as I can see, their legs are kind of "creepy." I get it.
- FEAR OF COMMITMENT: This one pops up before any big decision, not only marriage. It is not primarily the fear of the commitment, rather than the lie that you're binding yourself to something or someone you won't be able to get out of afterward.

How many of these do you struggle with? If they are honest, everyone struggles with fear to some degree, including myself. But in recent years, I have learned a strategy to overcome them. My desire to live life fully and freely far outweighs any perceived fear. So, how do I do it? How does one overcome fear? Well, first, you need to properly identify it.

The Bible says, in 2 Timothy 1:7, "*For God has not given us a spirit of fear, but of power and love and of a sound mind.*" Fear is a SPIRIT. That is important. When I learned that fear is a spirit, I realized it needs to be dealt with spiritually. Now, if you grew up a Christian or have a faith-based upbringing, this may not sound weird. I totally understand why you might be perturbed about this if you don't. However, whether you believe it does not make it less true.

The next thing you need to identify in your journey to overcome fear is its origin. When in your life did this fear to take root?

## UNLEASHED, by Justin Ford

Let me tell you a story. I watched many shark movies growing up, and I subsequently carried a considerable fear of the ocean for many years. This was sad because the ocean is one of the things I love the most. It is one of my favorite places to be, but I would never dare take a step further into it than chest level. I went down to a friend's house in Fort Lauderdale a few years ago. My buddy, Corey, had a boat, and one evening he took me out on the ocean.

Another friend, Jeff, had lived in Florida all his life. He was with us too. While we stopped to fish, Jeff climbed to the boat's top, took off his shirt, and back flipped into the ocean. I almost peed my pants. I could not believe what he was doing.

I guess my face revealed my shock, because he was trying to reassure me how safe it is, how he has gone snorkeling in these areas before, and how he's even swam with sharks. I did not want to hear more. I just could not understand how he would jump in if he knew there may be sharks in the area. I was fully expecting to witness a scene out of those childhood movies.

Instead, Jeff and Corey had a great time. They even invited me in a few times. Truth is, I desperately wanted to experience the ocean the way they were. I would have loved to jump off the boat and put on some snorkeling gear. I thought to myself, would I even be afraid of the ocean if I had never watched those shark movies? What are the real chances I get eaten by a shark? I did not know, and at the time I wasn't willing to take even an infinitesimal chance. I firmly parked my behind in the boat.

Maybe you can relate to my story. Maybe it is not sharks, but maybe perhaps flying on an airplane? I used to fear this too. Again, like the ocean, traveling is one of my favorite things to do. I have been all over the country and for many years, once the plane got up in the air and we started to experience turbulence, I would literally pray for God to spare my life! It was terribly intense until those bumps would stop. My body was paralyzed by fear and the thought of the plane crashing in the middle of the ocean and getting eaten by a shark was NOT how I wanted to die. Like the ocean however, I knew I needed to face these fears head-on.

But, what is fear again? A spirit. And how do you overcome a spirit? By looking to God and His Word. Trust what God says and stand up to it. Renew your mind on it daily.

## CHAPTER 4 PRINCIPLE FOUR - FREEDOM FROM FEAR

As I write this chapter on fear, we're on lock-down due to the Coronavirus pandemic. Our governor signed a statewide executive order telling everyone they must stay home. The fear that has gripped the globe is staggering. People are stuck and afraid. Unfortunately, when fear is the cause, we usually look at the worst-case scenario.

Faith is the opposite of fear. Faith is trusting in God, His (God's) Word, and things hoped for. One thing I have learned is that faith and fear cannot coexist, and there is no middle ground. You cannot have faith and also walk-in fear at the same time. You must choose which one you will serve, faith or fear.

Last night, my family and I watched a movie about the prophet Daniel in the Old Testament of the Bible. If you have not read the book of Daniel, or watched the movie, I strongly encourage you to do so. There are several stories from that book that demonstrate how having faith and trust in God overcomes fear. Here is one of my favorites, it's the story about Shadrach, Meshach, and Abendego.

For this reason at that time certain Chaldeans came forward and brought charges against the Jews. They responded and said to Nebuchadnezzar the king: "O king, live forever! You, O king, have made a decree that every man who hears the sound of the horn, flute, lyre, trigon, psaltery, and bagpipe and all kinds of music, is to fall down and worship the golden image. But whoever does not fall down and worship shall be cast into the midst of a furnace of blazing fire. There are certain Jews whom you have appointed over the administration of the province of Babylon, namely Shadrach, Meshach and Abendego. These men, O king, have disregarded you; they do not serve your gods or worship the golden image which you have set up." Then Nebuchadnezzar in rage and anger gave orders to bring Shadrach, Meshach and Abendego; then these men were brought before the king. Nebuchadnezzar responded and said to them, "Is it true, Shadrach, Meshach and Abendego, that you do not serve my gods or worship the golden image that I have set up? Now if you are ready, at the moment you hear the sound of the horn, flute, lyre, trigon, psaltery and bagpipe and all kinds of music, to fall down and worship the image that I have made, very well. But if you do not worship, you will immediately be cast into the midst of a furnace of blazing fire; and what god is there who can deliver you out of my hands?"

Can you even imagine being threatened to immediate death by blazing fire? Talk about an opportunity to be fully paralyzed by fear! But rather than fear, hear the response they gave. Shadrach, Meshach and Abendego replied to the king, *"O Nebuchadnezzar, we do not need to give you an answer concerning this matter. If it be so, our God whom we serve is able to deliver us from the furnace of blazing fire; and He will deliver us out of your hand, O king. But even if He does not, let it be known to you, O king, that we are not going to serve your gods or worship the golden image that you have set up."*

What an answer! That is how you fight the spirit of fear! The faith these three young men displayed is truly epic. In the face of certain death, they trusted and had faith that God was greater than the king, greater than the fiery furnace, and that He would deliver them. But they even trusted in God's judgment enough that if He chose not to save them, they still would not give in. (Spoiler alert! God saved them!)

Let me summarize the rest of the story for you. So, the King does not take kindly to their reply and commands his guards to heat up the furnace seven times hotter than normal. He wanted to "make an example" of them. Once the furnace was ready, they were bound up, carried up the steps and tossed in. The furnace was so hot, the guards who threw them in died. But the three didn't. The King was shocked. He asked his guards to remind him how many men they threw in. He said, *"Didn't we throw in three men? I see four walking around in there, and the fourth one shines like the son of a god!"* Yup! God showed up! And He's GREATER than any fear or threat that you are facing.

I overcame my fear of both flying and the ocean in a similar way, although not quite as epic. I put my faith and trust in God and went for it. God is our safety. So the next time I hit turbulence, I reminded myself of this truth and continued to breath. When I was in Florida a few months after my first visit with Corey, we went out on the ocean again and I jumped off that boat (mind you, I immediately swam back to the boat, but it was still a victory)!

## CHAPTER 4 PRINCIPLE FOUR - FREEDOM FROM FEAR

So what about you? Want to stop allowing fear to rule over you? Are you ready to begin living in freedom the way God planned and intended? Then take authority over the spirit of fear and trust in God!

I want you to remember this when fear tries to rear its ugly head again; this is what fear stands for:

- **F**alse
- **E**vidence
- **A**ppearing
- **R**eal

That's it! Fear is false evidence. And it is NOT real! The spirit of fear is a bully. It will try to intimidate you, and lie to you. But fear is no match for God!

*(Now, here is where I feel I need to add a little disclaimer: Fear is not real, it is a lying spirit—but DANGER is very real. Do not, under any circumstance, willfully put yourself in any dangerous situation in the name of "faith." That is not faith—that's called testing God. And it is plain foolishness. Do not be a fool.)*

So, it is decision time. If you're ready to stop allowing fear to control you, then follow the exercise below.

## Exercise

Write out every fear that you struggle with. Even if it's small—let's get rid of them all. Then, I want you to think back to where each fear started; identify the origins and contributing factors of this fear. Then, write out what Frightens out about it. You will see, it's not actually the fear itself. Next, list the best—and worst-case scenarios of you facing your fear. Finally, do research on your fear. Find some real statistics on the odds of your worst-case scenario materializing. You will see—the odds will be next to nothing, meaning for all intents and purposes, next to impossible. Once that is all done, I want you to pray a prayer. Not just any prayer—model it after the example below. Find a quiet and private place to pray. Be bold! If you need to yell it, then yell it! If you need to yell it many times, go ahead! This spirit of fear has not given you any peace—return the favor and berate it until it flees!

## Example

- **Fear** -  Flying on airplanes
- **Source** - Hearing about plane crashes, seeing all those pictures and videos of wreckages on the news. Watching families cry.
- **What frightens me about this** - Dying/Dying in a frightening way.
- **Best Case Scenario** - I get on and off the plane with no issues. I get to where I am going.
- **Worst Case Scenario** - The plane crashes and I die.
- **The Statistics say** - Air travel is statistically the safest form of travel. The likelihood of the plane crashing and everyone dying is 1 in 5.4 Million (or, 0.00000019%). Someone online wrote, "If you've safely made it to the airport, you've already made it through the most dangerous part of air travel."

## Prayer

*God, thank You that You have not given me a spirit of fear but of Power and of Love and of Sound Mind. As David prayed to you in Psalms 34:7, "and you delivered Him from all his fears," I ask you to deliver me too.*

*I put my faith and trust in you and acknowledge that you are greater than (place a description of the fear here), and I rebuke the spirit of fear over my life right now in Jesus' name Amen!*

# CHAPTER 5

# PRINCIPLE 5
# UNDERSTAND & TRUST THE PROCESS

## Definition

*Process*—a series of actions or events performed to make something or achieve a particular result; a series of changes that happen naturally; proceeding or moving forward; progressive course.

## Bible Verse

*"Consider it a sheer gift, friends, when tests and challenges come at you from all sides. You know that under pressure, your faith-life is forced into the open and shows its true colors. So don't try to get out of anything prematurely. Let it do its work so you become mature and well-developed, not deficient in any way."*
(James 1:2-4 MSG)

*Grapes must be crushed to make wine. Diamonds form under pressure. Olives are pressed to release oil. Seeds grow in darkness. Whenever you feel crushed, under pressure, pressed, or in darkness, you are in a powerful place of transformation.*
– Lalah Delia

## The Story of Joseph
(Source: brief paraphrase of Genesis chapters 37-50)

This is the story about a young man named Joseph. His father's name is Jacob, and they lived in Canaan. Joseph was seventeen (old enough to drive a car these days), and he had eleven brothers; and only one was younger than him. Can you imagine having eleven brothers to play with, or fight with?

**UNLEASHED,** by Justin Ford

Because Joseph was one of the youngest, his father spent more time with him, and he became very special to his father. So special that Jacob had a robe made for Joseph. (They did not have jackets back then, so think of this like a cool and expensive jacket). It was very beautiful and had every color on it you could imagine. All of Joseph's older brothers saw this and they got very jealous. They got so jealous they could not even be nice to him anymore.

One day, Joseph had a dream. He went and told his brothers, "Hey guess what?! Last night, I had the coolest dream. We were tying up bunches of grain out in the field when suddenly my bunch stood up, while all of yours gathered around and bowed to mine." The brothers looked at each other in disgust, but Joseph barely noticed, and continued, "then I had another dream that the sun, moon, and eleven stars bowed down to me."

"Who do you think you are?" the brothers said. "Do you think that you are better than all of us? Do you think that we would ever bow down to you?"

This made the brothers dislike Joseph even more. When he told Jacob about it, his father said, "Those are indeed strange dreams." But he thought carefully about what Joseph had told him.

A few days later Joseph's father asked him to check on his brothers. They were in the fields quite a distance away. Joseph did as his father asked. When the brothers saw Joseph in the distance, they made a plan to kill him. But when Reuben, Joseph's oldest brother heard of the plan, he said, "Let's not kill him, just throw him in a well out here in the field." Reuben said this because he was secretly planning to come back and rescue Joseph.

When Joseph arrived, the brothers ambushed him. They removed his robe and threw him down an empty well. A little while later, a group of traders passed by. They were on their way to Egypt. One of the brothers spoke up, "Why don't we sell him to these people? This way we never have to see him again, and we don't have to kill him." The others liked this idea, and they sold him to the traders.

Unfortunately, Reuben had not seen what happened and when he'd returned, Joseph was gone. The rest of the brothers took Joseph's beautiful robe and dipped it in animal blood. They took it

# CHAPTER 5 PRINCIPLE FIVE - UNDERSTAND AND TRUST THE PROCESS

back to their father. When Jacob saw it he cried, "Some animal has killed my son!" He wept for many days, so much that nobody could comfort him.

Now, while Joseph had started out as a slave in Egypt, the Lord was with Joseph and He helped him in every situation. Joseph had been sold into the household of Potiphar, an assistant to the Pharaoh. Potiphar saw that Joseph had aptitude and eventually put him in charge of everything in his house. After a false accusation from Potiphar's wife, Joseph was sent to jail. Even in jail, the Lord was with Joseph, and Joseph was promoted even among the prisoners.

After Joseph had been in jail for many years, Pharaoh's cup-bearer and baker were sent to prison too. One night, they both had vivid dreams. They recounted their dreams to Joseph, because God had given Joseph the gift of dream interpretation. He told the cup-bearer he would soon be let out of jail.

Joseph asked of him, "please tell Pharaoh about me when you're released, I need to leave this place." But when the cup-bearer was freed he promptly forgot and went about his business. Joseph stayed in jail for an additional two years.

One night Pharaoh had a disturbing dream. Nobody in his court could interpret it for him, and this brought him great distress. The cup-bearer then remembered Joseph and Pharaoh immediately summoned him from prison.

"Can you understand dreams?" Pharaoh asked.

"I cannot," was Joseph's reply, "but God helps me."

After Pharaoh narrated his dream, Joseph explained, "God is warning you. There will be seven years of plenty followed by seven years of severe famine, where nothing will grow."

"What can be done?" Pharaoh asked.

"God has warned you with sufficient time if you act now." Joseph replied, "Beginning now and for the next six years, Pharaoh must save a portion of the harvest. Once this is collected it should be enough to sustain Egypt through the seven years of famine."

Pharaoh agreed and placed Joseph in charge of executing the plan. He, in an instant, went from being a prisoner to second-in-command in all of Egypt. Joseph then began, the plan God had revealed to him.

Two years into the famine, people were coming from far and wide to purchase grain from Egypt—including Joseph's brothers. He recognized them, but they did not know who he was, after all, it had been almost twenty years.

The brothers all bowed before him—just as he had dreamed. He was an important man now, second only to Pharaoh. After a few meetings, Joseph could not keep it a secret any longer. He cried out to his brothers, "I am Joseph! Is my father alive?!" His brothers couldn't answer him. They were too afraid.

Joseph assured them saying, "Come here. I am your brother. Do not worry, and do not be angry at yourselves for selling me, because God put me here to save our people from starving."

Eventually Joseph's father, all his brothers and their families came to live in Egypt with Joseph. They had all the food they needed and grew into a large nation.

\*\*\*

Process. It is one of the most important key principles on our journey. It is in the process we truly become all that God has created us to be. As a matter of fact, there is only one road headed to where you're going, and it is called Process Highway. It is one lane - straight ahead. Everyone who has fulfilled their purpose has patiently traveled this highway, and everyone that has not decided to exit. This highway is littered with obstacles, roadblocks, detours, and storms. None of them are there by accident, and God will use them all to prepare you for your purpose and assignment.

What I love about the story of Joseph is the detour—that is not really a detour. God spoke to Joseph when he was very young, in a dream. He received a vision of the outcome, not the process he Would have to endure to get there. Then, after sharing the dream—likely with a tinge of pride—Joseph quickly gets thrown into a pit, sold into slavery, sold again, and thrown into prison (on false charges) to waste away and be forgotten. It looks like a huge detour on the surface, but he was right on track. God allowed for it all.

Let's back up for a moment though, can you imagine being thrown into prison for doing nothing wrong? Joseph did the right thing by refusing the sexual advances of his boss' wife and STILL went to jail!

## CHAPTER 5 PRINCIPLE FIVE - UNDERSTAND AND TRUST THE PROCESS

While it is not in scripture, I am sure there were times when Joseph questioned God's vision and purpose for his life, and maybe even His presence in all this. Have you ever asked God similar questions?

Joseph did not know that his 14 years of hardship were actually 14 years of preparation. Contrary to what he may have believed, he was not on the highway to hell—he was on the highway of process. See, God was building Joseph's character for the amount of responsibility he was to receive. As my pastor, Apostle Ellis Smith says, you cannot pray for character, and it is not a spiritual gift. Character can only be built and developed through difficulty and the testing of your faith.

To me, the most moving part of the story of Joseph is when his brothers arrive in Egypt. All the pieces start coming together again, and God's master plan begins to become visible. When Joseph's brothers arrived, they dutifully bowed down before the "man in charge." They had no idea they were standing before Joseph but can you imagine what was happening in Joseph's heart? He was watching his dream come to pass, and while it is not explicitly mentioned in the scripture, I know he was moved emotionally.

From what we've already learned about bitterness and unforgiveness, we can safely assume Joseph had already forgiven his brothers. After all, there is no way Joseph could have ruled over Egypt seething with bitterness. He did, however, put his brothers through multiple tests. Before you judge him too harshly for that, remember that as second-in-command of Egypt, he had incredible power. At his word, Egyptian guards would have wrangled up his brothers and swiftly carried out any revenge scenario Joseph could imagine.

The real victims (if we want to use that term) were all his scheming brothers. Can you fathom the depths of guilt they carried?

Can you imagine the look of fear on their faces when they realized who he was? Before Joseph revealed his identity, the brothers whispered to each other in their native language. They did not know Joseph understood. They were throwing accusations at one another, assuming they finally paid the price for what they did to their brother years ago.

But God is not petty—His plans are much larger and have a breadth and depth we just can't understand. He lives outside of time. He called Joseph to command Egypt in order to save the budding nation of Israel from starvation and nestle them in the most prosperous land in the world (at the time, Egypt). Imagine if Joseph had given up during his time of testing? The short answer is that the world would have starved and few would have survived if any. But the long and involved answer is that without going through the PROCESS, the promise of your purpose will NEVER come to pass.

Everyone who desires to fulfill their purpose must submit to the process. The same God that charted the life-course of Joseph charts out yours. You may not be a King or Queen. You may not experience famine or rule a nation. Those are just details and circumstances, but the fundamentals entirely apply to you and your life.

Learning about the process and Joseph's story has become crucial to my own process. It has given me hope. It has shown me that no matter what I face, God is using the situation to build the character, wisdom, and experience necessary to fulfill His purpose in my life. I have experienced times of such intense hardship and suffering I was sure that God had forgotten about me. Shortly after getting married, Joy and I bought a home, a few new cars and thought we had arrived financially after a few prosperous years in business. We began to travel, eat out and do a lot of unnecessary spending. Joy and I were never taught anything about money or debt, so we racked up some debt and thought that big commission checks would last forever. Boy, were we wrong. Before we knew it, the economy was collapsing, and within a few months, we went from six figures to no figures overnight. We lost both of our cars to repossession, our house to foreclosure, filed bankruptcy, got on food stamps, had to move our family of five into my mom's house, and slept on her basement floor.

I felt like a failure and didn't understand why we had to go through hard times. But as difficult as those times were and as hard as it is sometimes to go back there mentally and relive some of those memories—I have a different perspective. I know now you cannot get to your purpose without going through the process, and I learned so much from that period, and it prepared Joy and me to now be responsible for the success we have and teach others about the process we had to go through.

## CHAPTER 5 PRINCIPLE FIVE – UNDERSTAND AND TRUST THE PROCESS

Once I understood this verse, it completely changed my life:

*Count it all joy and consider it a sheer gift, friends,*
*when tests and challenges come at you from all sides.*
*You know that your faith-life is forced into the open under pressure*
*and shows its true colors.*
*So don't try to get out of anything prematurely.*
*Let it do its work, so you become mature and well-developed,*
*not deficient in any way.*
(James 1:2-4 MSG)

So, from today forward, I want you to write this verse down and COUNT IT ALL JOY when you find yourself in tough times. I want you to remember Joseph when you feel like giving up. I want you to commit TODAY that giving up is not an option. The world needs you to fulfill your purpose. You have been given a specific assignment that only you can achieve. Submit to the process and let God mold you into all He created you to be.

Lastly, God will use you to encourage others along the way. This is a great gift and encouragement. You will be able to share what you have learned and bring them comfort and hope when they are in similar circumstances. I have truly learned how to embrace the process, and I encourage you to do the same.

## Exercise

I want you to sit down in a quiet place. Quiet places are important—I hope you are noticing the trend here. In this peaceful place, I want you to write down the times in your life that were very hard and difficult.

I want you to look back at those times and write down what your thoughts and feelings were that you were experiencing. Did you feel lonely? Abandoned? Afraid or lost? Did you imagine you would never get through it?

Then, write down what you learned from those moments. What did you take away from those times? Did they help you build character? Give you fresh wisdom? Make you stronger?

How have these things shaped you to become the person you need to become to fulfill your purpose?

It is important to reflect on these times and not miss the lessons. You've got to purposefully continue along your Process Highway and *Count It All Joy*.

## Example

| | |
|---|---|
| Hard time: | Going through bankruptcy and foreclosure |
| What was I feeling? | I was afraid to lose everything and be homeless. |
| What did I learn? | That my wife and I did not have the wisdom or experience (at the time) to know how to properly manage our finances. |
| The Take-away? | Not to get myself in debt anymore, and to manage my finances well. |

How did this help me towards fulfilling my purpose? A part of God's vision and purpose for my life is to teach people how to become successful, build wealth and be good financial stewards. Without going through this, I would not have learned the lessons I needed to learn in order to become successful myself and teach others to do the same.

## Connect

Lastly, I want you to pray the prayer below and then post on your social media.

## Prayer

*God, Thank You that You have a perfect plan for me and thank You for the process that You are taking me through so that I can become the person that I need to be to fulfill Your purpose in my life. From today forward I make a commitment to submit to the process and make a decision to count it all joy. In Jesus' Name, Amen!*

### Social Media Exercise

If you've made it this far, I know that you're committed to making a change and I want to be part of your journey!

Post the following on social media and make sure to tag me:

"*I am committed to the Process #unleashedbook #countitalljoy*"

You can find me here. Also make sure to join our "Unleashed" Facebook community @ Unleashed Book by Justin Ford-Community.

Facebook -  @theofficialjustinford
Instagram –  @theofficialjustinford

Please also subscribe to my podcast by visiting www.justinfordpodcast.com or by searching the "Justin Ford Unleashed Podcast" on Apple, Spotify, Google, and Sounder.

# CHAPTER 6

# PRINCIPLE 6
# MENTORSHIP & ACCOUNTABILITY

## Definition

*Mentorship*—relationship between two people where the individual with more experience, knowledge, and connections is able to pass along what they have learned to a more junior individual within a certain field or area of life.

## Bible Verse

*"Without consultation and wise advice, plans are frustrated. But with many counselors/mentors they are established and succeed."*
(Proverbs 15:22 AMP)

*Show me a successful individual and I'll show you someone who had real positive influences in his or her life. I don't care what you do for a living—if you do it well I'm sure there was someone cheering you on or showing the way. A mentor.*

— Denzel Washington

## The Power of Mentorship
(Paraphrase from, Source: brightside.me/wonder-people/the-tough-story-of-michael-oher)

Michael Oher was a large, quiet, and unassuming teenager. He was an absolute fire on the football field, and his life—while having a rough start—inspired the movie, The Blind Side (I recommend you watch it). Oher's life is a lesson in effort and empathy, and that is why I'd like to share it with you.

## UNLEASHED, by Justin Ford

In 2002, in Memphis, Oher was practically homeless. Oher's father had passed away, and his mom had substance abuse issues. At 16 years old, Oher struggled through school while coming in and out of foster care—he was effectively homeless. With the help of school administrators, Oher was able to attend Briarcrest Christian School. There, he received help to raise his grades. His gifting was very obviously athletics, and the coach of the football team had an incentive to raise his grades high enough to play and participate in extracurriculars. Sean Tuohy, a wealthy and successful Christian businessman, had two children attending Briarcrest. He often would cover the tuition and lunch debt for struggling families and visit the school to speak with the principal. Tuohy was made aware of Oher's situation and decided to help.

With the help of teachers, Oher's grades had improved enough for him to begin participating in sports. He excelled considerably on the field and helped the football team win many games. Many families, including the Tuohys, would take him in for a few days a week as his housing situation had not yet changed.

One specific evening after practice, Mrs. Tuohy offered him a lift home. Upon seeing his difficult living conditions, she decided it would be best to offer Oher a place with her family. This would be the first time he confessed to the family. He would have his own bed.

With his housing situation finally settled, Oher was finally in a position to properly focus on his grades and bring them up to a level where he could qualify for college. Before the Tuohys, the college had not been thought or possibility for Oher. Five days a week, Mrs. Tuohy tutored Oher after school and helped him to organize his schedule. Progress was slow, but sure enough, with the support of the Tuohy family, Oher graduated. The ceremony was very emotional for all those who had a part in his journey, and the whole school and community were very proud.

Oher was accepted to the University of Mississippi and in 2009 graduated with a degree in Criminal Justice. He also played college football, and upon graduation, signed a five-year, 13 million dollar contract with the Baltimore Ravens. In 2013, the Ravens won the Super Bowl.

## CHAPTER 6 PRINCIPLE SIX - MENTORSHIP AND ACCOUNTABILITY

Oher's story is a shining example of how with perseverance, mentorship, and support, no obstacle is insurmountable.

\*\*\*

Mentorship is a vital part of God's plan for you to succeed and fulfill His purpose in your life. Plain and simple, we are not meant to figure it out on our own. I would not be where I am in my life today if it wasn't for the many mentors, advisors, and counselors that I have and have had since becoming a Christian at 19 years old.

A mentor, advisor, or counselor is simply someone that comes into your life to help teach you, guide you and hold you accountable. They allow you to become who God has created you to be. I can relate a lot to Michael's story. We both come from a rough background, and I got into lots of trouble. I can say without a doubt that without my mentors and advisors, I would have been a lost cause.

As you can see in the key verse for this chapter,

*"Without consultation and wise advice, plans are frustrated. But with many counselors (mentors) they are established and succeed."*
(Proverbs 15:22 AMP)

God placed the Tuohy's in Michael's life to provide wise counsel, which helped him establish his plans. They helped him stay on the right track and taught him things he needed to know. Michael did not have to allow the Tuohy's to help him. He just as quickly could have turned them down or been standoffish. But Michael wanted to better himself, his circumstances, and his future and willingly accepted the help.

It's important to note this—some individuals are hesitant to accept help or feel like they need to go at this alone. That is not true. You are not a "charity case" for accepting help when offered. Mentorship is a choice. It is wise to seek out and allow mentors, advisors, and counselors into your life. If you desire to fulfill God's plans for your life, mentors are essential. I have mentors, advisors, and counselors for all the different areas in my life. What does that look like? Well, I have spiritual mentors (pastors), financial advisors, business mentors, success mentors (some call them life coaches), a marriage counselor, and a health & fitness mentor (personal trainer). I believe, as you can see, it is very important to have a myriad of counselors/mentors in your life.

If you truly desire for your plans to succeed, you should get a mentor or advisor in that area. It does not necessarily need to be a formal or paid arrangement. But having a second set of more experienced eyes on your situation and progress can save you a lot of time and unnecessary frustration.

You have the ability to climb out of your current circumstances and create the life you envision. You are not limited to the circumstances you were born into either. Align yourself with like-minded individuals and find people who are where you want to be in life.

What I love about the Bible, especially the book of Proverbs, is the incredible wisdom it contains. King Solomon, the author of Proverbs was the son of King David (you know, the one who killed Goliath. If you are not familiar with the story, look it up, it's epic). So, after the passing of his dad, Solomon prayed and asked God for wisdom to rule the people of Israel. God granted him his request.

Solomon was and remains the wisest person ever to live. Throughout Proverbs, Solomon references the importance of surrounding yourself with wise counsel. Even as a King—the wisest King—he did not push aside his advisors. At every level, we can benefit from teachers. We all need individuals in our lives that can counsel, instruct, and correct us when necessary. God often sends mentors, counselors, and advisors into your life. Pay attention, so you don't miss out!

As mentioned in the introduction of my book, my first mentor entered my life two days after I checked myself into the Grace Centers of Hope. It was back in May of 2002, and I was 19 years old. On that particular day, Dwayne and his family walked through the doors. I had no way of knowing at that moment just how impactful he would be in my life. Dwayne was in his early 40s and from the inner city. We did not immediately hit it off, but I was willing to hear more once he opened up about his life and struggles. Dwayne grew up in a Christian household, but he made deplorable choices that resulted in a drug addiction early on. Both he and his wife hit rock bottom and, like me, came to Grace Centers looking to change their lives.

Dwayne knew so much about the Bible and God. I was brand new to everything in the faith, and I knew very little. On a daily basis, Dwayne would teach me the Bible, pray for me and encourage me if I was feeling down. He believed in me and took me under his wing. I became like his little brother and felt like a part of his family. I cannot express just how important his friendship and mentorship were to me as I started my life all over again—it was invaluable.

Dwayne shared a Bible verse with me one day. It remains one of my favorites and what I consider to be absolutely foundational in my faith walk. Romans 8:28 (NASB) and says, *"And we know that God causes all things to work together for good to those who love God, to those who are called according to His purpose."* This verse has helped me through various trials in my life since. I thank God that He sent Dwayne into my life for that season.

God is very intentional about when He sends mentors. I am still very close to some, while others have been for a specific situation or season. I have noticed that if you pay attention, God sends the right individuals at the appropriate time. Now, not every mentor will seek you out—many you will have to seek out yourself. Others you may have to hire, as a coach or nutritionist. I currently have three coaches for different areas in my life. I pay for their service and time monthly, and it is absolutely worth it.

Regardless of where you are in your journey, I pray and recommend you do as well for God to send mentors into your life. May He also give you the wisdom to identify them. Some will be good teachers, but if you are sensitive, you'll feel a tug in your soul to begin to pursue this individual as a mentor.

In seeking a mentor, you first want to be sure their character, integrity, and values align to where God is taking you. You want to make sure they walk their talk—and not just talk. Beware of those—there are many.

Attending my first church, once out of the center, I met Pastor Pat. He was such an incredible godsend. I treasure to this day the lessons he taught me about how to be a Man of God, walk with integrity, and how to be a Godly daddy to my then 2-year-old daughter. He gave me a chance and invested in me when no one else would. Pastor Pat had patience and gave me his full attention when I had questions. I was (and still am!) so appreciative and truly respected his advice. He's always given me great advice, he confirmed my choice of Joy to be my wife and married us later that year!

Pastor Pat has been part of my life and our children's lives ever since. To this day, I meet with him regularly. He is probably the most influential mentor I have had, and I can say with confidence, I wouldn't be the man I am today if God hadn't brought him into my life.

There have been so many mentors across different areas in my life I feel like I could fill a whole book with just those experiences, and my gratitude (hey, there's an idea!). As I share with you now though, I want to mention my current Real Estate Coach, Kate Simon.

I first met Kate years previously but was reacquainted with her at a Glover U Real Estate convention in January 2019. During the convention, it became painfully apparent that I was not performing to my potential professionally. I had a great mentor early on in my real estate career, Mr. Jeff Glover, but I had not developed as strongly as I could have since leaving his team. I immediately approached Coach Kate, the Head Coach of the Glover U Organization, and laid out to her my needs and goals.

She was 100% confident she could help, so I hired her on the spot! She truly is the best of the best, and hiring her remains one of my wisest business decisions to date. She is full of energy, enthusiasm and truly is a no-nonsense butt-kicker! She helped me transform my real estate business and continues with weekly checkups to keep me focused and accountable (and kick my butt when needed). To understand the power of a coach and mentor, Kate helped me go from selling $5,000,000 before I hired her, to selling over $30,000,000 in just two years. Yeah, I would say hiring her was worth it!

Study any successful individual—any—and I guarantee you will find strong mentors in their past. My mentor, Jeff Glover, said it best, "No one succeeds alone." I know that, and I am a living example. I would not be who I am, where I am, or have achieved the success I have today without each and every mentor.

That said, I'd like to take a minute to honor said mentors, advisors, and counselors. You have all had a unique impact on my life, and I am forever grateful: Dwayne Lyons, Dr. Mike Stoltenberg, Kymosh Myrick, Pastor Ray Anderson, Pastor Dave Arnold, Pastor Art Ledlie, Pastor Pat Bossio, Jr., the late Bishop Ben Gibert, Apostle Ellis Smith, Sal Lacaria, Dan Cadez, Shawn Williams, Bonnie Pile, Kate Simon, Jeff Glover, Monique Carter, Scott McGlaughlin, Pastor Jack Hickey, Pastor Alex Lappos, Greg Yackley, Tiffany Jones, Sabrina Adams, Pastor Mark Dunlap, Mrs. Char Dudek, Eric, and Cindy Moore, Dr. James Foster and my late Grandpa, John J. Murphy. I also give pre-emptive thanks to those mentors I have yet to meet. I'm genuinely looking forward to it.

So now, let's put together a game plan to help you identify and find some mentors in your life.

## EXERCISE

What areas in your life are you lacking leadership, and what areas can you benefit from having a mentor? Here are seven key areas where you will want to have mentors, advisors, and counselors:

- **Spiritual** – Someone that can help teach you and guide you, such as a pastor, ministry leader, or someone who has been walking in faith longer than you.
- **Business** – Someone that can teach you how to succeed in your line of business.
- **Marriage/Family** – Someone to teach you and show you how to be a great spouse and parent.
- **Financial** – This could be to get out of debt, how to build wealth, how to be a good steward.
- **Health & Fitness** – Could be a trainer at the gym, a meal planning coach or anyone to help you accomplish your health goals.
- **Career/Occupation** – Someone who can teach you how to

succeed in your job or career.

- **Life in General** – Any area of life where you need help or guidance such as overcoming an addiction, strengthening your mindset, school/education, or need a counselor during a life crisis.

Once you have identified the areas you need a mentor I want you to pray the prayer below, keep your eyes open, and begin looking for your mentors. There is a saying, "**When the student is ready, the teacher will appear.**"

## PRAYER

*God, thank you for the wisdom of having many mentors, advisors, and counselors. Lord, please send me the mentors (advisors and counselors) to help me along my journey in becoming who You have created me to be. Open my eyes to see who those people are when they arrive. Give me the boldness to pursue. In Jesus' Name. Amen.*

# CHAPTER 7

# PRINCIPLE 7
# HUMILITY – THE DOORWAY TO DESTINY

## Definition

*Humility*—genuine gratitude, lack of arrogance, a modest view of one's self. Described in biblical terms, humility is a critical and continuous emphasis on godliness. Individuals are called upon to be humble followers of Christ and trust in the salvation of God.

## Bible Verse

*"Humble yourselves [with an attitude of repentance and insignificance] in the presence of the Lord, and He will exalt you [He will lift you up, He will give you purpose]."*
(James 4:10 AMP)

*True humility is not thinking less of yourself; it is thinking of yourself less.*

– Pastor Rick Warren

\*\*\*

**H**umility is one of those tricky words. It confuses people. But that is because most don't know it's true definition. Many confuse humility with humiliation, which is understandable because they share the same Latin root word but are very different.

Humiliation is a forced abasement of pride. It is not necessarily an emotion, though it's often confused with intense embarrassment. Instead, humiliation is an act of "putting someone in their place" or being "knocked down a peg or two." It is always preceded by pride and/or an overstep of importance or status.

## Now—Back to Humility

Humility can be defined as having a modest opinion of oneself or a fair estimate of one's own importance. It is a lack of pride, or even more simply, being down-to-earth. According to a study at Berkeley, humble individuals handle stress more effectively, report higher levels of mental well-being, and show greater generosity, helpfulness, and gratitude. Sounds great, right?!

So why does humility have such a bad rep? It has more to do with how we use and understand it of the opposite—of pride.

Now, before I delve into the definition of pride and why it is dangerous, I need you to know that I'm not talking about mom-is-so-proud-of-her-little-boy's-first-goal or I'm-so-proud-of-my-vegetable-garden pride. Often, that "pride" is simply gratitude or an acknowledgment of work well done. And that is perfectly fine! It is essential to acknowledge and celebrate those moments. But, technically speaking, "pride" is not the right word. I want to talk about original, Biblical pride— and believe me, it isn't pretty.

Pride (hubris, excessive pride or self-confidence) is the opposite of humility and goes beyond arrogance. Biblically, it is defined as overconfidence multiplied until dangerously out of control. Once out of control, it will spiral into self-will and foolishness. It is the polar opposite of acknowledging God and following His will. It is the spawn found in Lucifer's heart before he fell and became Satan—yeah, scary stuff.

Pride is arrogantly thinking. We do not need God's help or guidance. We walk through the life we are given, trying to create our own purpose and tread our own path without acknowledging the ONE who created and designed us in the first place.

Romans 2:4 says, *"Are you [actually] unaware or ignorant [of the fact] that God's kindness leads you to repentance [that is, to change your inner self, your old way of thinking—seek His purpose for your life]?"*

It was God's goodness and kindness that led me to a place of humility. It was and continues to be the best gift. Finally, being able to confess I did not have all the answers was incredibly liberating. I thought chasing money, girls, or social status would fulfill me—but it never did. After falling on my face over and over, I finally came to the conclusion that I needed God to save me. I needed actual divine intervention.

This was a humbling moment for me. I no longer felt like I was "the man." I needed God's help, and I was willing to hear and accept the truth. The truth is the person of Jesus Christ. He came to earth over 2000 years ago, died on the cross for my sins so that I could be saved and resurrected with Him to eternal life. In that one moment of humility, I realized I was a sinner. I was a broken man who asked Jesus to forgive me of my sins. The moment, I knew I needed a Savior. Jesus stepped into my life—immediately—and saved me.

At the time, I did not know what it all meant to be saved and have a relationship with Jesus, but I knew something was fundamentally different. I had nothing to lose and everything to gain. I had an empty and burnt-out life that He (Jesus) was willing to trade for.

So, what is Salvation, and what does it mean to be saved? "Sozo" is the Greek word for Salvation (saved, born again).

According to Strong's Concordance, the definition goes beyond our understanding of the remittance of sins. Sozo also implies physical healing, deliverance, and more. That means being freed from Satan and his demons in a spiritual sense.

Salvation, then, must mean more than simply being saved from sin to go to Heaven when you die. To be Biblically saved means much more. Biblical Salvation affects your daily life here-and-now. It's the pursuit of Christ-likeness, the ability to resist temptation and demonic attack, be free from the judgment and wrath of God, and receive healing in our physical bodies. There is more, and they're listed among the many promises of God in scripture. You really should check it out.

*"For God so [greatly] loved and dearly prized the world, that He [even] gave His [One and] only begotten Son, so that whoever believes and trusts in Him [as Savior] shall not perish, but have eternal life."* (John 3:16 AMP)

The Bible says, "today is the accepted time, today is the day of salvation," so how does one get saved?

The significance of Salvation can be symbolized as a doorway—a transition or passage from one place to another. That is what Salvation is, only it's not a place—it's a person. Jesus (Salvation) is the doorway to your destiny and the life God designed for you to have. Through Him you pass from death to life, darkness to light, lost to found, empty to overflowing!

> *"Amazing grace, how sweet the sound that Saved a wretch like me. I once was lost but now I'm found was blind but now I see."*
>
> – John Newton

Have you heard of John Newton? If not, then I am sure at some point you may have encountered the Hymn, Amazing Grace… you haven't? No worries! Go ahead and Youtube "Amazing Grace." Have a listen. Any version will do—they are all rather uplifting. Even more inspiring is the individual who penned these words.

John Newton grew up in a poor English household in the 1700s. His dad was a sailor, and his mom passed away when he was very young. He started sailing with his dad before the age of twelve and fell into some very filthy habits. Within ten years, he was commanding slave ships and had the reputation of being an incredibly profane (irreverent/disrespectful) individual.

This was John Newton before his encounter with Jesus—before his Salvation. After a nasty storm at sea and a near-death experience, Newton became far humbler and began his faith journey. A few short years later, he was a successful Pastor, family man, and pillar in his community. His words—a testament to the Salvation power of Jesus—still ring true over three hundred years later.

If you are not saved and have never asked Jesus to forgive your sins and invite Him into your life, I'm sure at some point you've sensed that something is missing or doesn't quite make sense. Or perhaps, like John Newton, you have lived through some scary and humbling experiences that are starting to make you question things deep down. The Bible says, *"we all have sinned and fall short of the Glory of God*" (Romans 3:23) and that every human being is born into sin and separated from God.

This, however, was not God's initial plan. When God created Adam and Eve, they were perfect. We have all heard the story (or some basic version) of Adam and Eve in the garden. Eve bit the apple in disobedience after being deceived (lied to) by Satan disguised as a serpent. Rather than trusting and obeying God, Eve was enticed by the idea of becoming "like God." Unfortunately, Adam took a bite as well. At that moment, their eyes were opened—but not as they thought. Their innocence was gone, and immediately sin was birthed into the world. Adam and Eve's sin has been carried by all humankind ever since.

We witness the effects of this brokenness daily in the world today. This does not mean everyone who isn't saved, is stuck in addiction or gross depravity, but it does mean the unsaved individual can never live their life the way God designed. Their purpose will remain unfulfilled.

Every day individuals pursue what they believe will make them happy and fulfilled. There is nothing wrong with wanting to be satisfied—and I'm certainly not advocating for a life of misery. But my experience has taught me that happiness and fulfillment are not found in people, possessions, or careers.

One of the Bible verses I learned early on in my faith walk is Psalm 107:9 (NKJV). It says, *"For He (God) satisfies the longing soul and fills the hungry soul with goodness."* I can testify to how true and accurate this verse is. Only God can bring true satisfaction and fill that void we are all born with. God never intended us to be separated from Him. The only way to be brought back from the separation created by sin is to confess your sin. Acknowledge your need for a Savior and ask Jesus (the only One qualified to be an all-sufficient Savior) to save you and be your Lord.

This one singular decision "transformed" my life. This one vital decision restored my life. This one fateful decision made me whole, set me free from addictions, gave me abundant hope for the future, and transformed me into the man I am today. This one pivotal decision allowed me to have written this book so that at this moment in time and history, you can have the opportunity to do the same.

This decision has the power to turn your life around, to give you joy, to make you whole, to heal you, and establish you on the path to your purpose and destiny. This one decision truly has unlimited possibilities and immeasurable implications and can set a new precedence for all the generations to come after you.

Romans 10:13 (KJV) says, *"For whosoever shall call upon the name of the Lord shall be saved."* You are the "whosoever," and it does not matter how big your sins are or what you have done in your life. God can and WILL save you. If you humble yourself and call upon His name, He promises to save you!

Is your soul longing and hungry like Psalm 107:9 describes? Are you ready to become the person who God created you to be? Are you finally prepared to throw in the towel and admit your ways just have not worked out?

Yes? Good!

There is no greater honor than I've experienced in my life than that of introducing one to their Maker and witnessing a life-changing decision. If you are ready to take that step, then I'd like you to humble your heart right now and pray this prayer aloud:

## PRAYER

*Dear God, I am a sinner in need of a Savior, and I ask You to forgive me of my sins. Jesus, come into my life and be my Lord. Today I humble myself and confess that my way doesn't work, and from today forward, I choose to follow You. I confess You as my Lord and Savior and ask that You please fill me with Your Holy Spirit in Jesus' Name, Amen!*

Congratulations and welcome to the Kingdom (family) of God! You have just made your **GREATEST** decision ever!

By making the decision to accept and follow Jesus Christ, your life will NEVER be the same. The Bible says in Luke 15:10 (GNT), *"In the same way, I tell you, the angels of God rejoice over one sinner who repents."* How AMAZING! Angels in Heaven are literally rejoicing over your decision right now. You have got Heaven's attention!

I can feel God's Presence so strongly as I write this, knowing that potentially millions of individuals who read this book prayed this prayer will be in Heaven one day. WOW! I cannot express how excited I am for you, and all God has in store for your life.

With that being said, I would like to know about your decision today. I want you to reach out to me and let me know how I can pray for you moving forward. Make sure you join our Facebook Group @Unleashed Book by Justin Ford - Community. I want to be an encouragement along your journey in becoming all God created you to be.

## SOME BUSINESS…

Now that you've been saved, I want to recommend a few items to help you along.

- **First and foremost** —if you do not already have a Bible, get one. I recommend a hard copy and a Bible App called You Version.
- **Second**—find a good bible believing church in your area. Pray and ask God to help you find one.
- **Third**—pray to God daily. Prayer is a conversation. As you read the Bible, mix it with prayer. God will reveal Himself to you in a mighty way.
- **Lastly**—if this book has inspired you and made a difference in your life, then pass it along! I recommend giving this book to someone else you think needs to read it. Or better yet, buy another copy and give it away!

# CHAPTER 8

# BONUS PRINCIPLE 8 – THE SECRET WEAPON

### Definition

**Secret Weapon**—a thing or person which they believe will help them achieve something and which other people do not know about; something that gives you a special advantage.

### Bible Verse

*"So we fasted and petitioned our God about this, and He answered our prayer."*
(Ezra 8:23 NIV)

Fasting has been around for thousands of years. Many people fast for different reasons. Perhaps the first time you heard about it was when someone explained intermittent fasting for weight loss. By and large, however, fasting has been used traditionally for spiritual or religious purposes (fun fact! You still reap all the physical benefits of fasting even if you are doing it for spiritual reasons).

The Bible references fasting over 120 times. Often, in the Old Testament, God called His people to fast and pray. It was always for a specific reason, some of the reasons include going into battle, repenting of sin, or believing for a miracle. What is remarkable is that every time someone humbly followed the instructions of God they received their breakthrough.

After reading all those stories I could not help but realize that this was a secret weapon. God's heart is moved by fasting and prayer, and the supernatural is broken open. This inspired me to put it into action.

While writing this book I faced very trying times, truly the most trying times in my 38 years on this earth. Believe it or not, writing this book has taken two years. During this time, I've learned how to leverage the secret weapon for specific battles and seek answers. It has truly transformed my life!

When you fast, you're depriving your body (flesh) of a necessity—food/sustenance. Do not confuse it with starving yourself, you're not starving yourself or denying your body nutrients. Instead, you're purposefully turning to God during the time you would normally devote to eating and relying on His strength and sustaining grace. I remember the first time I completed a 24hr fast. It was difficult—but it forced me to focus and trust in God. The benefits far outweigh any discomfort during the process.

In the Bible, Jesus performed many miracles. He healed people of disease, cast out demons, walked on water, and even raised someone from the dead. Jesus lived a life of prayer and fasting. As a matter of fact, before He began His public ministry, Jesus fasted 40 days in the desert. He set aside that time to draw closer to God (His Father) and prepare Himself for what lay ahead.

During that time, the devil tempted Him to eat. Jesus understood the significance of His fast and obviously did not give in. When you fast and deny your body/flesh sustenance, it very quickly begins to "throw a fit." Your body is accustomed to receiving a certain number of calories at a certain time each day. Change that and you will quickly be hit with hunger pangs, headaches, and mood swings. That is normal though—because God created our bodies to eat and digest food. There is something in denying physical sustenance and turning to God that gets His attention.

Again, and again, the Bible tells us to fast, and yet so many Christians don't use this important key. I have learned that if you will humble yourself and obey God's instructions—believe Him—you will witness supernatural things take place in your life.

There are two types of fasts; the first you decide to begin yourself and the second when God commands you. I have completed both, and when God has called them in my life they've always been for a very specific purpose. I remember one morning waking up and hearing the Lord call for a fast. He did not immediately give a reason.

Since I had learned to simply obey the voice of God when He spoke, I fasted the full day and trusted. That evening, after I had returned from work, I found out why.

My brother-in-law burst into my house and said there was something seriously wrong with my sister. They lived next door at the time. I ran over immediately and found her lying face down on her bed. I asked her if she was okay. No answer. I sat down on the bed next to her, placed my hand on her back to reassure her, and asked again. She whispered back, "They're after me."

I asked, "Who's after you?"

As I asked, I could feel something moving under her skin, almost bulging. She said, "Someone was in the back seat of my car. They jumped on me and into my body." She started to shake and scream. Immediately, the Lord told me it was a demonic spirit and instructed me to pray in tongues until it left her. I prayed for several minutes. She eventually stopped shaking and screaming and began crying. I smelt an awful smell and thought my sister had soiled herself or something—it was that bad—but it was actually the spirit leaving her body. Yes, demonic spirits can carry bad odors, like sulfur. My sister had dabbled in witchcraft and opened the door for Satan and his demons to come into her life.

As I continued to pray God revealed to me this was the reason, He called me to fast that day. I remembered the bible passage in Mark 9:25-29 (NIV), "*When Jesus saw that a crowd was running to the scene, he rebuked the impure spirit. "You deaf and mute spirit," he said, "I command you, come out of him and never enter him again." The spirit shrieked, convulsed him violently, and came out. The boy looked so much like a corpse that many said, "He's dead." But Jesus took him by the hand and lifted him to his feet, and he stood up. After Jesus had gone indoors, his disciples asked him privately, "Why couldn't we drive it out?" He replied, "This kind can come out only by prayer and fasting."*

## Side Note

*The above story is not to frighten you. This may be the first time you are hearing first-hand about a Spiritual Warfare experience, and so I'd like to be sensitive to that. First, do not fear. You are covered in the blood of Jesus. Stay close to Him. If you still feel a little scared, sing praise songs until you are lost in worship, and do not forget that fear as we discussed earlier is a spirit and you have the authority over those spirits. Second, be careful what you watch and "open the door to." What do I mean by that? Nix those horror/thriller movies that incite fear and expose you to the occult, spiritual warfare, and demons are real. They are filthy beings and aren't to be messed with.*

Prayer and fasting open up a heavenly portal over you and you tap into the supernatural realm which is very real. If I had not obeyed God that day, I wouldn't have been able to help my sister. When you begin to fast yourself and experience the power that follows, you will also begin to know when to use it.

For additional reading, I highly recommend "Fasting" by Jentezen Franklin. It is a small book but very dynamic. Franklin describes the importance of fasting and shares many stories of miracles experienced by individuals who dared to fast and trust God. After reading his book my faith began to be stirred up as well. The Bible may have been penned thousands of years ago, but God honors His word. Today, if you will believe what He says, you too can step out in faith. Trust Him, and He will make a way for you!

As I mentioned at the beginning of this chapter, that the last couple of years has been the most difficult for me. The situation I faced looked next to impossible to survive. Between 2018-2019 I was named in multiple lawsuits stemming from a bad business partnership. I later had issues with an accounting firm that caused my taxes to be delayed. I racked up over $125,000 owed to the IRS. One of my businesses went from having 30+ employees and thriving, to dwindling down to 4. Finally, I fell behind on an office lease due to a drastic business decline. I owed $25,000 in back rent and another $60,000, if I could not fulfill the lease. As you can imagine, I felt backed into a corner. I was against the ropes and did not know what to do except trust God.

## CHAPTER 8 BONUS PRINCIPLE EIGHT - THE SECRET WEAPON

Early in 2018, I joined a new church. The pastor, several times a year, called for a corporate fast. The pastor several times a year would plan for the entire church to fast and pray together anywhere from four days or as many as ten days. It had been a while since I fasted for an extended period of time and was excited to fast with the church. The first time we fasted it was for four days, then longer periods. All of these were liquid-only fasts—no food. I felt a supernatural strength and began to see God make a way when there seemed to be no way.

In August of 2019, after going back and forth, the landlord of my office agreed to break our lease one year early under the condition we paid the $25k back-rent. Heading into the slowest season of real estate, I was not sure what would happen. But through fasting and prayer, God provided big time! We received enough income to pay off what we owed before any installments were due. Talk about a breakthrough!

Going into the following year, God began to speak to me about fasting for a breakthrough. He wanted me to fast for 30 days. The thought of this was intimidating, but I always knew at some point I would complete a 30-day liquid-only fast. I personally knew several Christians who fasted 30 days—it changed their lives. You might be thinking OMG there is NO WAY I can go 30 days with no food. Honestly, that is what I believed before too—but this was different. I decided to map out a plan going into the next year. I would fast seven days in January, ten days in February, 14 days in March, 21 days in April, and 30-days in May. New Year's Eve was very significant for me. I was at the altar praying to God and trusting Him to see His supernatural work in my life for the next year. I wanted to experience His breakthrough and see the list of challenges and debts overcome.

After fasting seven days in January and ten days in February, I began to experience some progress. The early winter months in real estate are always the slowest, mostly due to the weather in Michigan. Not that year—I sold so many homes in those two months and I knew it was a direct result of fasting and praying. I had great momentum going into March when COVID hit and like everything else, the real estate market shut down. There was a lot of uncertainty at that time, but I trusted God to be my anchor and held on.

I did not complete the 14 day fast in March that I had originally planned, but I did begin an online Bible study. It was a 31-day Proverbs challenge where I would go on Facebook Live and read aloud a chapter from Proverbs each day. At the end of each reading, I would ask for prayer requests and we would all pray together. We grew very close, did a five-day fast together, and witnessed breakthroughs and miracles.

The real estate market was scheduled to open back up in May. Days before, the Lord called me back to the 30-day fast. It was clear that I needed to humble myself to receive the promises that God had for me. Rather than feeling as if this was an impossible task, I was excited. I was believing God for miracles and I was ready to see God move supernaturally.

And guess what? He totally did!

That month (June), in addition to the fast I also completed another 31 day Proverbs challenge. June was incredible. Ten people gave their lives to Jesus and another ten rededicated their lives and personally, I sold 31 homes and exceeded my sales volume for the entire previous year. From the commissions alone I earned enough to pay off over $100k in various debts I had accumulated. I also purchased and remodeled a new home!

The 30-day fast in June took my life to a whole new level. I finished the year having doubled my income and having surpassed my yearly home sales goal by 10 percent—all during the pandemic. Talk about the supernatural!

I credit all the victory to God, and humbly obeying His call to fasting and prayer (my secret weapon).

As I am writing this chapter, at the beginning of the new year. Tomorrow, January 4th, we're beginning a 21 day fast as a church. I cannot wait to see all that God has in store for this year!

This chapter is not only to challenge you to incorporate fasting into your life but also to demonstrate to you how amazingly God can work when we obey. If you need a breakthrough or a miracle, remember that God does not play favorites. He will adhere to His promises and principles. If God has come through for me, He can and will for you too!

# IN CLOSING

There was a time in my life when many people wrote me off as a lost cause. Perhaps they have said similar things about you. But you need to know—God has not written you off, and neither have I. By applying these 8 key principles to my life, God has brought me from a drug-addicted and alcoholic high-school dropout with no job or vision to the man I am today. Now, I live on purpose! God has given me the grace and opportunity to write books, have a positive impact on people's lives and live a life full of vision and success. I'm married to an amazing woman, I've got four wonderful kids—and just recently, a grandson!…and no kidding, I feel like I'm just getting started.

When Jesus saved me in 2002, that is when my life truly began. Even now, daily God is still surprising me!

**To Recap the Eight Key Principles!**

- Purpose
- Vision
- Forgiveness
- Fear
- Process
- Mentorship
- Salvation
- Fasting

*It is my prayer that as you apply these 8 Principles, God will do for you (and greater!) than He has done for me. Your life, I firmly believe, will make an impact on the lives of others and generations to come. It may not be easy, but it will absolutely be worth it. One saying I live by (and always repeat to myself, just ask my wife), is quitters never win and winners never quit. Refuse to give up, and with these Godly principles, you WILL succeed!*

*I pray that this book has encouraged you and given you hope. Know that no matter what you have gone through, or no matter what you are going through, God makes ALL THINGS possible!*

**UNLEASHED**, by Justin Ford

*God, I pray that whoever reads this book will encounter Your power, Your anointing, Your Presence, and Your love. As they apply these Key Principles to their lives I pray that in the same way You have transformed my life, I pray that You would also transform theirs in an Even Greater Way. Lead them to experience an Unleashed life!*

*In Jesus' Name, Amen!*
*God Bless you and I just want you to know that I believe in you!*

*Justin Ford*
UNLEASHED

    I have written this book to share my story and the principles I have applied to transform my life. Writing this book wasn't easy, as I am not a writer by nature. Matter of fact. It took many years to get to this point. I can recall the first time I opened my laptop to start writing and after a few sentences I got frustrated and closed my laptop for almost ten years, until I opened it again to begin to write. I wrote this book because, first and foremost, God told me to and second because it is my prayer that this book can change someone's life, give them the hope necessary and look at my life as an example knowing that if God can change me, He can change you too! I pray that as you read the words of this book that God becomes as real to you as He became to me and that as you apply these principles that you would experience God's **Unleashing** Power in your life. It's an honor and a privilege to share my story with you and if my story blesses you and helps you in any way would you do me a favor and share it with someone else. Also please let me know as well how this book made an impact on your life.

God Bless you!

**UNLEASHED**, by Justin Ford

To order additional copies of *Unleashed*, visit Justin's website at www.justinfordunleashed.com.

 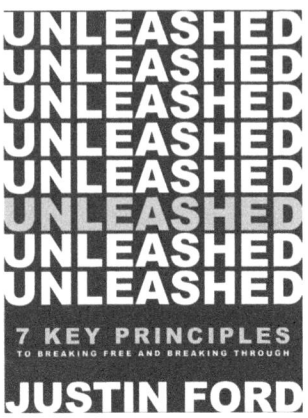